FUTURE OF WORK

Navigating the Post Pandemic Job Market

Geoffrey Zachary

CONTENTS

GEOFFREY ZACHARY

Future of Work: Navigating the Post-Pandemic Job Market

CHAPTER I.
INTRODUCTION

The Evolving Terrain of Employment

The employment landscape is witnessing a metamorphosis of unprecedented proportions. Ground-breaking technological strides, paired with shifts in global demographics and unforeseen challenges, are redefining our understanding of work. Gone are the days when career trajectories were linear and predictable. As the world grapples with the aftermath of a global pandemic, our workplaces, too, are bracing for change. This post-pandemic professional milieu emphasizes not just technical know-how but also adaptability and resilience. Automation, artificial intelligence, and remote work paradigms are altering job roles, demanding an updated skillset in response. Concurrently, demographic shifts, including an ageing workforce in many nations and a booming youth population in others, further complicate the equation. Individuals must now be agile learners, ready to pivot as industries evolve and job descriptions transform. Employers, on their part, must offer dynamic work environments that prioritize continuous learning and employee well-being. As we stand at the crossroads of tradition and innovation, one thing is certain—the future of work will be a tapestry of challenges and opportunities, demanding both foresight and adaptability from all stakeholders.

Ripple Effects: The Pandemic's Imprint on the Job Landscape

The COVID-19 pandemic, an unforeseen and unparalleled force, dramatically upended the global job market. As industries scrambled, some trends, like remote working and digital reliance, rapidly accelerated. Organizations, once reluctant to embrace remote arrangements, transitioned overnight, revealing both the potential and pitfalls of such setups. However, the pandemic wasn't just a technological disruptor; it spotlighted deeper socio-economic fissures. Sectors like tourism and hospitality faced stark downturns, leading to unprecedented job losses, while others, such as digital services and e-commerce, flourished. Moreover, the crisis underscored disparities; those with digital proficiency and remote-compatible jobs sailed relatively smoothly, whereas manual labourers confronted stark vulnerabilities. The mental toll of the pandemic also became evident as professionals grappled with blurred work-life boundaries, isolation, and burnout. As businesses reimagine post-pandemic strategies, issues of equity, mental well-being, and digital infrastructure take centre stage. The pandemic, in its devastation, has offered a chance to rebuild the job market with resilience, inclusivity, and adaptability at its core.

"Future of Work: Navigating the Post-Pandemic Job Market" is a lighthouse in these uncertain times, illuminating the intricacies of our evolving professional realm. Envisioned as a beacon, this book's core objective is to equip readers—be they individuals at crossroads in their careers, organizations recalibrating their work models, or policymakers drafting the next game-changing labour legislation—with knowledge and foresight.

"Future of Work" is not merely an academic exploration but a practical guide through the post-pandemic professional terrain. This book, divided into focused chapters, dissects the evolving job market, influenced by technology and pandemic-induced shifts. Key topics range from remote working, skills evolution, diversity, and entrepreneurship, to technology's pivotal role in transforming the workforce.

Through enlightening discussions, readers encounter the challenges and triumphs in this new work era, enriched by real-world examples that showcase innovation and adaptation. The content, concise and illuminating, dives into the intricate nuances of these changes.

Moreover, "Future of Work" empowers its audience. Individuals gain strategies for personal career navigation, organizations receive insights into digitization and nurturing resilient cultures, and policymakers glean understanding for forward-thinking legislation. In this new world of work, while challenges are rife, opportunities also abound. The book emphasizes that our individual and collective decisions will define work's trajectory. With informed choices, adaptability, and evolving skillsets, we can prosper in the reshaped job landscape.

CHAPTER II.
UNDERSTANDING
THE POST-PANDEMIC
JOB MARKET

Navigating the New Norm: Job Market Evolutions:

The reverberations of the pandemic echo loudly within the realm of job trends and industries. With the enforced lockdowns and safety concerns, technology rapidly advanced from being an aid to a necessity. We witnessed a shift from conventional to digital, and automation became more than just a buzzword. As the world grappled with the virus, industries like hospitality and travel faced setbacks, with reduced demand leading to job contractions. Conversely, the healthcare sector, e-commerce, and tools facilitating remote work surged forward, carving out stronger spaces in the global economy.

Consider the transformative journey of e-commerce. Quarantines led to a surge in online shopping, revealing the latent potential of this industry. Giants like Amazon quickly seized the moment, scaling up their logistics and fulfilment capacities. The outcome? A substantial spike in hiring to accommodate the rise in online purchases. This scenario exemplifies the evolving nature of work. For job seekers and professionals, these changes emphasize the essence of flexibility, continuous learning, and the ability to pivot.

Recognizing and riding these waves of change can spell the difference between career stagnation and success in this recalibrated job market.

The Virtual Revolution: Workplace's Digital Evolution

COVID-19 acted as a catalyst, propelling organizations into the future. The concept of a traditional office underwent a metamorphosis as companies globally were nudged into exploring remote work's viability. Driven by the need to maintain business continuity while ensuring employee safety, digital tools became the sinews binding teams together. Video conferencing, cloud solutions, and collaborative platforms turned into daily essentials, necessitating workers to hone their digital proficiencies.

An illustrative testament to this seismic shift is the approach of tech giants like Twitter and Shopify. Embracing the "work from anywhere" mantra, they transitioned to permanent remote work structures. Beyond just a logistical decision, this heralded a profound transformation in the job landscape. By decoupling job roles from locations, these companies tapped into a geographically diverse talent reservoir, unhindered by borders. For workers, this means newfound freedom and a broader spectrum of opportunities.

In essence, the digital transformation spurred by the pandemic isn't merely about technological adoption—it's about reshaping organizational cultures, redefining career paradigms, and expanding horizons in the world of work.

Mastering the Post-Pandemic Skillset

As we transcend the aftershocks of a global pandemic, the job marketplace unfurls a canvas painted with new nuances. This landscape is rich with opportunities but demands a specialized set of skills and competencies. The essence of what employers seek has seen a notable transformation. While tech-savviness in data analytics, digital marketing, and cybersecurity stands strong, an equal weightage is placed upon softer skills that chisel a professional's versatility.

The World Economic Forum, in its 2020 report, underscored critical thinking, problem-solving, and creativity as beacons for future employability. The report's sentiments resonate with LinkedIn's 2021 findings which prioritize digital fluency, effective communication, and collaborative attributes, among others. The pattern that emerges highlights a craving for individuals who are not just technically proficient but are agile thinkers and harmonious collaborators.

Adapting to these recalibrated expectations demands an intentional effort. Aspirants must view their career as a continuum of learning, perpetually updating their repertoire and diversifying their skill set. The emphasis should be on holistic development that marries technical acumen with interpersonal effectiveness.

Companies, on the other hand, shoulder the responsibility of nurturing this ecosystem. By investing in upskilling programs and fostering a milieu that champions continuous learning, they can bridge the skill gap. Such endeavours not only empower employees but position companies as forward-thinking entities in the post-pandemic world.

Policymakers to play a cardinal role. By harnessing insights from the evolving job arena, they can shape policies that amplify workforce readiness, thereby fostering economic vitality.

In summation, navigating the complexities of the post-pandemic job market isn't just about seeking a job; it's about understanding the shifts, imbibing the necessary skills, and above all, being malleable in approach. Our future at work is a symbiosis of technical prowess and soft skill mastery, underlined by an unyielding spirit of adaptability.

On the flip side, while companies like Zapier have harnessed technology for seamless remote collaborations, some firms grapple with ensuring effective communication across virtual teams. Moreover, while some employees relish the autonomy of remote work, others miss the camaraderie of an office environment, leading to feelings of disconnection. Therefore, while remote work offers substantial flexibility and broader talent access, its success rests on addressing the inherent challenges to ensure a harmonious and productive work environment.

However, the challenges are not to be underestimated. The lack of physical presence can hinder team cohesion and the serendipity that arises from casual office interactions. Many employees report feeling disconnected, which can impact morale and productivity. Moreover, the overlap of personal and professional spaces can lead to burnout, as people find it hard to "switch off" from work. Cybersecurity is another concern, with employees accessing company data from various networks.

While companies like Trello and Slack offer tools that facilitate virtual collaboration, building a company culture remotely requires deliberate effort. Regular check-ins, virtual team-building activities, and clear communication protocols become essential. It's a balance—while the remote model presents undeniable advantages, both employers and employees need to actively address its challenges to reap its full benefits. As the world tilts further towards remote work, understanding and navigating these dual aspects become crucial for the future of work.

CHAPTER III.
ADAPTING TO
REMOTE WORK

Benefits and Challenges of Remote Work

The modern working landscape, post-pandemic, has witnessed a transformative shift towards remote work. The benefits of this model are immediately apparent. Firstly, employees can relish the flexibility, freeing themselves from the daily commute and achieving a better work-life balance. This has also globalized talent acquisition; companies can now recruit from a worldwide talent pool, unhindered by geographical constraints.

However, the transition to remote work isn't without its challenges. The absence of physical interactions can cultivate feelings of isolation among employees. The demarcation between professional tasks and personal chores becomes hazy, leading to potential burnout. Such an arrangement also requires a heightened sense of self-discipline and robust time-management skills.

Pioneering companies like Automattic have championed the remote work model, showcasing its viability. Their success underscores the potent advantages of remote work. Yet, the challenges—ranging from team cohesion to cybersecurity concerns—require proactive strategies. As tools like Slack and Zoom bridge communication gaps, organizations must also foster a resilient and inclusive remote culture. The future of work is undeniably leaning towards remote models, and our ability to balance its pros and cons will dictate its success.

Strategies for Effective Remote Collaboration and Communication

As remote work becomes more prevalent in the post-pandemic era, robust collaboration and communication are paramount. The absence of physical proximity necessitates proactive strategies to bridge gaps and keep teams aligned. Digital tools, ranging from video conferencing software like Zoom to project management platforms like Asana, have become essential in this new landscape. Through them, real-time interactions, brainstorming sessions, and updates can occur seamlessly.

The key to a thriving remote team is establishing consistent communication patterns. Regular check-ins, whether daily stand-ups or weekly reviews, ensure everyone is on the same page. Clearly defined roles, expectations, and deliverables prevent misunderstandings and bottlenecks. Furthermore, a transparent environment where team members can voice concerns, share feedback, and celebrate achievements fosters trust and cohesion.

The rise of platforms such as Slack during the pandemic underscores their importance in facilitating effective remote collaboration. Beyond just text communication, they provide channels for sharing files, integrations with other software, and creating a virtual office environment. As the workplace continues to evolve, the emphasis on refining and optimizing remote collaboration strategies becomes increasingly significant. In this digital era, the tools are abundant; it's the strategy and execution that determine success.

Maintaining Work-Life Balance in a Remote Setting

Remote work, a trend accentuated by the pandemic, has become a central part of our professional lives. With its rise, the challenge of striking a work-life balance has taken on a new dimension. When our homes double up as offices, it's easy for work to bleed into personal time and vice versa. Thus, it's essential to consciously delineate boundaries.

Designating specific areas for work helps create a mental distinction between professional and personal spaces. Following a structured routine, akin to a traditional office day, reinforces this boundary. This involves regular start and finish times, punctuated by breaks. Similarly, "switching off" post-work hours – by turning off work notifications or shutting down the work laptop – helps in mentally clocking out.

Employers have a significant role in ensuring their remote workforce doesn't succumb to burnout. By championing a culture of well-defined work hours, facilitating regular check-ins, and emphasizing mental well-being, companies can foster a conducive remote work environment. Incorporating "no meeting" zones or offering wellness programs are initiatives that companies can undertake.

The beauty of remote work lies in its flexibility. It presents an opportunity to redesign how we approach work, giving precedence to productivity over hours spent. It's no longer about being tied to a desk but about delivering value. For individuals, this translates to greater autonomy in structuring their day, potentially allowing for better work-life integration.

Organizations benefit too. Beyond reduced overheads, they can access a global talent pool, ensuring diversity and innovation. There's a macro perspective as well, with the potential for reduced urban congestion and environmental benefits as fewer people commute daily.

In conclusion, as remote work cements its position in the professional world, maintaining a work-life balance becomes more about mental compartmentalization than physical separation. It's about working smart, leveraging flexibility, and remembering to unplug. As we navigate this domain, a concerted effort from both employees and employers is vital for sustainable success.

CHAPTER IV.
RESKILLING AND UPSKILLING FOR THE FUTURE

The Importance of Continuous Learning

In today's fast-paced world, standing still is the equivalent of moving backwards. Nowhere is this more evident than in the job market of the post-pandemic era. The landscape of work is shifting under the dual pressures of technological innovation and a globalized economy, making continuous learning no longer a luxury but a necessity.

The digital age brings with it an ever-evolving set of tools and skills. To remain relevant, professionals must be proactive in updating their knowledge and abilities. This lifelong learning mindset allows individuals not only to keep up with their industries but to anticipate and leverage changes for career advancement.

COVID-19 intensified this paradigm, underscoring the value of adaptability. With the pandemic causing unprecedented disruptions, many found themselves in positions where upskilling or reskilling became imperative to career survival. Consequently, e-learning platforms like Coursera, LinkedIn Learning, and Udemy saw a spike in enrolment, indicating a collective push towards self-improvement and adaptability.

In conclusion, continuous learning is the cornerstone of professional resilience and growth in the 21st century. Embracing this ethos is key to navigating the ever-changing waters of the modern job market and ensuring long-term career success.

Identifying Transferable Skills and New Areas of Growth

In an ever-shifting job market, the key to career longevity and success often lies not just in specialized knowledge, but in one's ability to identify and harness transferable skills. These skills, which can traverse industries, are a testament to an individual's adaptability and breadth of expertise. Critical thinking, leadership, and communication, among others, serve as assets in virtually every professional arena.

Furthermore, a proactive approach to recognizing and capitalizing on emergent trends is equally paramount. With the advent of the Fourth Industrial Revolution, technology is reshaping traditional industries at a staggering pace. Take, for instance, the ascent of AI and automation. They're not just creating new roles but transforming existing ones. Therefore, a marketer or financial analyst today could greatly benefit from understanding data analytics, transforming their career trajectory.

To navigate the modern professional landscape, individuals must therefore do two things: first, pinpoint and hone those skills which, regardless of industry shifts, will remain perennially valuable. Second, be agile and receptive to learning, ensuring they're well-positioned to seize emerging opportunities in the constantly evolving world of work.

Accessing Online Learning Platforms and Resources

In the digital age, the availability of online learning platforms has revolutionized professional development. These platforms serve as gateways to a vast array of courses, tutorials, and educational materials, providing individuals with convenient and flexible access to invaluable knowledge and skills. From coding and digital marketing to project management and entrepreneurship, the opportunities for learning and growth are boundless.

Massive Open Online Courses (MOOCs) such as edX and Khan Academy have emerged as trailblazers in online learning. By offering free or affordable courses from renowned universities and institutions worldwide, they have democratized education. Learners can now acquire industry-relevant skills at their own pace, from anywhere in the world.

In the post-pandemic job market, reskilling and upskilling have become imperative for professional success. Continuous learning expands individuals' skill sets, showcasing their adaptability and commitment to growth. By identifying transferable skills and exploring new areas of growth, individuals position themselves for emerging job opportunities and stay ahead of industry trends. Online learning platforms provide accessible and flexible resources, empowering individuals to take control of their career development.

The potential applications of reskilling and upskilling are vast. Individuals can make successful career transitions, enhance their current skill sets, or even embark on entrepreneurial endeavours. Employers can play a pivotal role by offering training programs and investing in their employee's professional development, creating a skilled and agile workforce. Governments and educational institutions can collaborate to provide accessible and affordable reskilling initiatives, equipping individuals with the tools to adapt to the ever-changing job market.

As the job market evolves, reskilling and upskilling are essential strategies for individuals to future-proof their careers. By embracing continuous learning, leveraging online platforms, and accessing a wealth of resources, individuals can navigate the post-pandemic landscape with confidence. The online learning revolution has opened doors to endless possibilities, empowering individuals to seize new opportunities for growth and success.

CHAPTER V.
LEVERAGING TECHNOLOGY IN THE WORKPLACE

Accessing Online Learning Platforms and Resources

In the digital age, the availability of online learning platforms has revolutionized professional development. These platforms serve as gateways to a vast array of courses, tutorials, and educational materials, providing individuals with convenient and flexible access to invaluable knowledge and skills. From coding and digital marketing to project management and entrepreneurship, the opportunities for learning and growth are boundless.

Massive Open Online Courses (MOOCs) such as edX and Khan Academy have emerged as trailblazers in online learning. By offering free or affordable courses from renowned universities and institutions worldwide, they have democratized education. Learners can now acquire industry-relevant skills at their own pace, from anywhere in the world.

In the post-pandemic job market, reskilling and upskilling have become imperative for professional success. Continuous learning expands individuals' skill sets, showcasing their adaptability and commitment to growth. By identifying transferable skills and exploring new areas of growth, individuals position themselves for emerging job opportunities and stay ahead of industry trends. Online learning platforms provide accessible and flexible resources, empowering individuals to take control of their career development.

The potential applications of reskilling and upskilling are vast. Individuals can make successful career transitions, enhance their current skill sets, or even embark on entrepreneurial endeavours. Employers can play a pivotal role by offering training programs and investing in their employee's professional development, creating a skilled and agile workforce. Governments and educational institutions can collaborate to provide accessible and affordable reskilling initiatives, equipping individuals with the tools to adapt to the ever-changing job market.

As the job market evolves, reskilling and upskilling are essential strategies for individuals to future-proof their careers. By embracing continuous learning, leveraging online platforms, and accessing a wealth of resources, individuals can navigate the post-pandemic landscape with confidence. The online learning revolution has opened doors to endless possibilities, empowering individuals to seize new opportunities for growth and success.

Embracing Digital Tools and Platforms for Productivity

In today's post-pandemic job market, the widespread adoption of digital tools and platforms has reshaped the way we work. From remote collaboration to project management and communication, these tools have become indispensable for enhancing productivity and efficiency in the modern workplace.

Project management platforms such as Asana and Trello have revolutionized team coordination. These tools provide a centralized hub where tasks can be assigned, progress can be tracked, and deadlines can be met. By streamlining project workflows and eliminating manual coordination efforts, teams can work together seamlessly and optimize their productivity. Additionally, these platforms offer features like notifications and integrations with other tools, ensuring that everyone is on the same page and can easily access relevant information.

Communication tools like Slack and Microsoft Teams have become essential for remote teams. They provide instant messaging, file sharing, and video conferencing capabilities, enabling real-time collaboration and efficient communication. These platforms facilitate quick decision-making, foster cross-functional collaboration, and bridge the physical distance between team members. With the ability to create dedicated channels and host virtual meetings, teams can maintain effective communication, regardless of their physical locations.

Moreover, cloud storage and document collaboration tools like Google Drive and Microsoft SharePoint enable teams to access and collaborate on files in real time. This eliminates version control issues and ensures that everyone is working on the most up-to-date information. By centralizing document storage and enabling simultaneous editing, these tools streamline workflows and enhance productivity.

Embracing digital tools and platforms is no longer a luxury; it's a necessity in today's fast-paced and interconnected world. Companies that leverage these tools gain a competitive advantage by optimizing their operations, fostering collaboration, and empowering employees to work more efficiently. Individuals who adapt and become proficient in these digital tools enhance their marketability and ability to thrive in the evolving job market.

In conclusion, digital tools and platforms are powerful resources for boosting productivity and efficiency in the post-pandemic job market. By embracing these tools and leveraging their capabilities, teams and individuals can work more effectively, collaborate seamlessly, and stay ahead in an increasingly digital and interconnected world.

The Role of Artificial Intelligence in the Future of Work

Artificial intelligence (AI) is poised to reshape the future of work, offering opportunities for automation, data-driven insights, and enhanced decision-making. Understanding the capabilities and potential applications of AI is crucial for individuals and organizations to adapt and thrive in this evolving landscape.

AI-powered chatbots are increasingly utilized in customer service, providing quick and efficient responses to routine inquiries. These bots free up human agents to focus on more complex customer issues, improving overall service quality and efficiency.

The potential applications of AI in the workplace are vast. By embracing automation and understanding its impact, individuals can proactively adapt their skills to align with emerging job requirements. Embracing digital tools and platforms enhances productivity and collaboration, enabling individuals to work effectively in remote or hybrid work environments. Leveraging AI technologies empowers individuals to automate repetitive tasks, gain valuable insights from data, and make more informed, data-driven decisions.

However, it is essential to address potential challenges and ethical considerations associated with AI adoption. The displacement of certain jobs due to automation requires a focus on reskilling and upskilling to ensure a smooth transition for affected workers. Ethical considerations surrounding data privacy, algorithmic bias, and responsible AI usage must be prioritized to create an inclusive and fair future of work.

As technology advances, individuals and organizations must embrace its potential and stay updated on new developments. By leveraging technology, individuals can enhance their skills, productivity, and overall work experience. Organizations that embrace digital transformation and integrate AI technologies will gain a competitive advantage in the post-pandemic job market. The effective utilization of automation, digital tools, and AI will shape the future of work, opening doors to new opportunities for success and fostering a culture of innovation.

CHAPTER VI. GIG ECONOMY AND FREELANCING

Rise of the Gig Economy and Its Implications

The gig economy has witnessed remarkable growth in recent years, with the COVID-19 pandemic further accelerating its expansion. This labour market, characterized by short-term contracts, freelance work, and independent contractors, offers individuals flexibility and autonomy in their work arrangements. However, it also presents unique challenges and considerations.

Platforms such as Uber, Lyft, and TaskRabbit exemplify the gig economy's impact. They have revolutionized the way people find and offer services, connecting individuals seeking transportation, home services, or odd jobs with freelance workers available on demand. This model has disrupted traditional industries and created new avenues for work and income generation.

The gig economy's rise has implications for both workers and the broader economy. On one hand, it provides individuals with the opportunity to choose their working hours, take on multiple gigs simultaneously, and enjoy the freedom of being their boss. This flexibility can be particularly attractive to those seeking work-life balance or supplemental income.

However, the gig economy also brings challenges. Gig workers often lack benefits such as health insurance, retirement plans, and job security. They assume the risks associated with irregular income and limited legal protections. Furthermore, the classification of gig workers as independent contractors raises concerns about labour rights, fair compensation, and social safety nets.

As the gig economy continues to expand, policymakers and businesses face the task of balancing the benefits of flexibility with the need for worker protection. Regulations and policies need to adapt to ensure fair treatment, access to benefits, and adequate labour standards for gig workers. The emerging discussions around employment classification and gig worker rights highlight the significance of finding solutions that address the unique dynamics of this evolving labour market.

In conclusion, the rise of the gig economy has transformed the way people work and earn income. It offers individuals flexibility and autonomy but also poses challenges related to worker rights and benefits. As the gig economy evolves, stakeholders must address these implications and strike a balance between flexibility and worker protection to create a fair and sustainable future of work.

Freelancing as a Career Option

Freelancing has emerged as a viable career option for professionals, providing them with freedom, flexibility, and a diverse range of projects. It allows individuals to showcase their expertise, build a dynamic portfolio, and have control over their workload and schedule. However, pursuing a career as a freelancer requires self-discipline, self-promotion, and the ability to navigate a constantly evolving market.

Freelancers, such as writers, graphic designers, and software developers, often work on a project basis for multiple clients. They have the freedom to choose the projects they want to work on and set their rates, granting them control over their careers and the opportunity to explore various industries and projects. This flexibility enables them to balance their personal and professional lives and pursue work that aligns with their passions and interests.

One of the benefits of freelancing is the ability to build a diverse portfolio. Freelancers can work with clients from different industries and gain valuable experience across various projects. This not only enhances their skill set but also increases their marketability and opens doors to new opportunities.

However, freelancing also comes with its challenges. Freelancers are responsible for finding clients, managing client relationships, and marketing their services. They must constantly update their skills and stay informed about industry trends to remain competitive. Additionally, freelancers face irregular income, as project-based work can have fluctuations in workload and payment schedules. It requires financial discipline and the ability to plan for lean periods.

Despite the challenges, freelancing offers numerous benefits and can be a rewarding career choice for those who are self-motivated and enjoy the flexibility it provides. With the rise of remote work and digital platforms, freelancing has become increasingly accessible and appealing to professionals across various industries.

In conclusion, freelancing has transformed into a viable career option that offers individuals freedom, flexibility, and the opportunity to work on diverse projects. While it requires self-discipline, self-promotion, and adaptability, freelancing provides professionals with the ability to shape their careers according to their interests and goals. By embracing the challenges and opportunities of freelancing, individuals can forge a successful and fulfilling path in the ever-evolving world of work.

Navigating the Challenges and Benefits of Gig Work

Gig work, characterized by flexibility and independence, presents both challenges and benefits that individuals must navigate. While freelancers often face income uncertainty, inconsistent workloads, and limited access to traditional employment benefits, the gig economy also offers opportunities to build a diverse skill set, network with professionals across industries, and gain exposure to different types of work.

For instance, gig workers with in-demand skills such as web development, digital marketing, or content creation can command higher rates and attract a steady stream of projects. By establishing a strong reputation and leveraging online platforms, these individuals can position themselves as industry experts and attract clients from around the world.

To successfully utilize the gig economy and pursue freelancing, individuals need to adapt their skills, manage their finances, and cultivate a strong professional network. Embracing technology and online platforms can facilitate connections with potential clients, showcase work samples, and streamline administrative tasks.

However, it is important to acknowledge the potential downsides of gig work, including the lack of job security, the need for self-motivation and discipline, and the responsibility for managing taxes and retirement planning. Government regulations and policies play a crucial role in ensuring fair treatment and protection for gig workers.

Navigating the gig economy and freelancing successfully requires an entrepreneurial mindset, adaptability, and effective self-management. Staying informed about industry trends, continuously developing skills, and cultivating a strong professional network is essential for thriving in this evolving job market.

Ultimately, the gig economy and freelancing offer individuals the opportunity to create a flexible and dynamic career path. By embracing the benefits, addressing the challenges, and leveraging technology, individuals can navigate the gig economy and freelancing landscape to find fulfilment, financial stability, and professional growth in the post-pandemic job market.

CHAPTER VII.
BUILDING A
PERSONAL BRAND

Importance of Personal Branding in a Competitive Job Market

In today's post-pandemic job market, personal branding plays a vital role in differentiating oneself and establishing a strong professional reputation. It involves creating a compelling and authentic image that showcases an individual's skills, expertise, and unique value proposition. Personal branding allows individuals to stand out from the competition, attract opportunities, and build credibility with employers, clients, and peers in their industry.

For example, a marketing professional who consistently shares valuable industry insights, actively engages with relevant online communities, and demonstrates their expertise through thought leadership articles and social media content will be perceived as a knowledgeable and reputable authority in their field. This enhances their professional brand and increases their visibility to potential employers or clients.

Building a strong personal brand requires individuals to identify their unique strengths and attributes and effectively communicate them to their target audience. This includes developing a professional online presence through platforms like LinkedIn, maintaining a consistent and cohesive personal brand message across all communication channels, and actively networking and building relationships within their industry.

By investing in personal branding, individuals can shape their professional narrative, control how they are perceived, and increase their chances of success in a competitive job market. It not only helps individuals showcase their expertise and stand out from the crowd but also allows them to align their values and aspirations with their chosen career path.

Furthermore, personal branding is not limited to job seekers. It is equally important for professionals who aim to advance in their current roles, attract new clients, or explore entrepreneurial opportunities. A strong personal brand enables individuals to build trust, establish credibility, and create a positive reputation that can lead to new opportunities and professional growth.

In conclusion, personal branding has become essential in today's competitive job market. By effectively crafting and managing their brand, individuals can differentiate themselves, attract opportunities, and build credibility in their respective fields. Embracing personal branding allows individuals to take control of their professional narrative and position themselves for success in an increasingly digital and interconnected world.

Developing a Strong Online Presence and Professional Network

In the digital age, developing a strong online presence and professional network is crucial for personal branding and career success. Leveraging platforms like LinkedIn, professional blogs, and social media allows individuals to showcase their skills, experiences, and achievements to a wide audience. Building a robust professional network enables individuals to connect with like-minded professionals, industry influencers, and potential collaborators.

For instance, an aspiring graphic designer who actively participates in online design communities shares their portfolio on platforms like Behance and engages in networking events or conferences will establish connections with fellow designers, potential clients, and employers. This network can provide valuable opportunities for collaboration, referrals, and job prospects.

To develop a strong online presence, individuals should optimize their LinkedIn profiles, regularly update their professional blogs or websites with relevant content and engage in meaningful conversations on social media platforms related to their industry. By consistently sharing valuable insights, contributing to discussions, and showcasing their work, individuals can establish themselves as experts in their field and attract attention from potential employers, clients, or collaborators.

Building a professional network involves actively connecting with industry professionals, attending conferences, joining professional associations, and participating in online communities. Engaging in networking events, both in person and virtually, allows individuals to establish meaningful connections, exchange ideas, and gain valuable industry insights.

A strong online presence and professional network can lead to a range of benefits. It opens doors to new opportunities, facilitates knowledge sharing and learning, and provides a support system of like-minded professionals. Additionally, a robust network can offer mentorship, collaborations, and referrals that can accelerate career growth and advancement.

In conclusion, developing a strong online presence and professional network is essential for personal branding and career success. By leveraging online platforms and actively engaging with industry professionals, individuals can showcase their expertise, connect with valuable contacts, and access new opportunities. Embracing these strategies allows individuals to expand their reach, enhance their visibility, and build a strong professional reputation in the digital landscape.

Showcasing Skills and Expertise through Digital Platforms

In the digital era, individuals have access to a wide array of digital platforms that allow them to showcase their skills and expertise in various formats such as blogs, videos, podcasts, and online portfolios. By consistently creating high-quality content that aligns with their niche and target audience, individuals can effectively demonstrate their knowledge, problem-solving abilities, and creativity.

For example, a software developer who regularly shares coding tutorials and open-source projects on platforms like GitHub or creates informative videos on YouTube will not only enhance their brand but also attract the attention of potential employers or clients who are impressed by their skills and commitment to sharing knowledge.

To utilize digital platforms effectively, individuals should develop a content strategy that focuses on their strengths and aligns with their career goals. Engaging with the audience through comments, discussions, and social media interactions can further establish their expertise and build credibility within their field. Additionally, adapting the personal brand to suit different platforms and target audiences ensures that the content resonates with the intended viewers or readers.

In the post-pandemic job market, employers and clients increasingly rely on digital platforms to evaluate potential candidates. A well-crafted personal brand that showcases skills and expertise can significantly influence hiring decisions and provide individuals with a competitive edge. By investing time and effort into building a strong personal brand, individuals can expand their professional network, attract opportunities, and navigate the evolving job market with confidence.

However, it is important to remember that personal branding is not about self-promotion or vanity. It is about creating a compelling narrative that showcases one's unique value and expertise. Authenticity, professionalism, and consistency are crucial in building a strong personal brand that resonates with the intended audience.

In conclusion, digital platforms provide individuals with powerful tools to showcase their skills and expertise. By strategically curating and sharing their work and knowledge, individuals can establish a strong personal brand that helps them thrive in the post-pandemic job market. Embracing digital platforms effectively enables individuals to enhance their professional reputation, attract new opportunities, and stay ahead in an increasingly digital and competitive landscape.

CHAPTER VIII.
ENTREPRENEURSHIP
AND START-UPS

Exploring Entrepreneurial Opportunities in a Post-Pandemic World

The post-pandemic job market has witnessed a surge in interest in entrepreneurship as individuals seek greater control over their professional destinies. Entrepreneurship offers the potential for innovation, flexibility, and the opportunity to create a unique path. It involves identifying market gaps, developing creative solutions, and taking calculated risks to build a successful business.

For example, during the COVID-19 pandemic, many individuals recognized the growing need for contactless delivery services. Entrepreneurs seized this opportunity and established successful start-ups offering innovative last-mile delivery solutions, leveraging technology and customer-centric approaches.

Entrepreneurship allows individuals to shape their futures and pursue their passions. It provides the freedom to explore new ideas, disrupt traditional industries, and make a meaningful impact. Moreover, it enables individuals to create their work environment and culture, fostering a sense of fulfilment and autonomy.

However, entrepreneurship also comes with its challenges. Starting a business requires meticulous planning, resource allocation, and the ability to navigate uncertainties. It involves wearing multiple hats, from marketing and finance to operations and sales. Building a successful venture requires resilience, adaptability, and a willingness to learn from failures.

In the post-pandemic world, opportunities for entrepreneurship abound. The pandemic has exposed new needs, accelerated digital transformation, and created an environment ripe for innovative solutions. By identifying market gaps and leveraging emerging trends, individuals can develop unique business ideas that cater to changing consumer demands and preferences.

Furthermore, technology has levelled the playing field, enabling aspiring entrepreneurs to access resources, connect with global markets, and build scalable businesses. Online platforms, crowdfunding, and digital marketing tools have democratized the entrepreneurial landscape, allowing individuals to start and grow businesses with relatively low barriers to entry.

In conclusion, exploring entrepreneurial opportunities in a post-pandemic world offers individuals the chance to shape their destinies and pursue their passions. It requires a combination of creativity, resilience, and strategic thinking. By identifying market needs, developing unique solutions, and leveraging available resources, individuals can embark on the rewarding journey of entrepreneurship and contribute to economic growth and innovation in the post-pandemic job market.

Building a Successful Start-up and Navigating the Business Landscape

Starting a business requires careful planning, market research, and a strong understanding of the target audience.

Entrepreneurs must develop a viable business model, define their value proposition, and create a roadmap for growth. Additionally, navigating the complex business landscape involves understanding legal requirements, marketing strategies, financial management, and building a strong team.

For example, Airbnb, a start-up that disrupted the hospitality industry, began with the simple idea of renting out air mattresses in founders' homes. Through strategic planning, innovative technology, and effective marketing, Airbnb evolved into a global platform connecting travellers with unique accommodations and experiences.

Building a successful start-up requires a combination of vision, determination, and execution. Entrepreneurs must identify a problem or opportunity in the market and develop a solution that adds value to customers. Thorough market research helps validate the business idea and understand the target audience's needs and preferences.

Developing a sound business model is critical for long-term success. This involves identifying revenue streams, cost structures, and a clear path to profitability. Entrepreneurs must also create a compelling value proposition that differentiates their business from competitors and resonates with customers.

Navigating the business landscape involves understanding legal requirements and regulations specific to the industry. Entrepreneurs must ensure compliance with licensing, intellectual property, and tax obligations. It is also important to implement effective marketing strategies to build brand awareness, attract customers, and drive sales.

Financial management is a key aspect of building a successful start-up. Entrepreneurs must develop accurate financial projections, secure funding, and effectively manage cash flow to sustain operations and fuel growth. This requires financial literacy and the ability to make informed decisions based on data and market trends.

Finally, building a strong team is essential for a start-up's success. Entrepreneurs must recruit talented individuals who share their vision and possess the necessary skills to execute the business plan. Effective leadership, communication, and collaboration are vital in fostering a culture of innovation and achieving business objectives.

In conclusion, building a successful start-up and navigating the business landscape requires careful planning, strategic thinking, and the ability to adapt to changing circumstances. By developing a viable business model, understanding legal requirements, implementing effective marketing strategies, managing finances diligently, and building a strong team, entrepreneurs can increase their chances of success in the competitive business world. With passion, resilience, and a customer-centric approach, entrepreneurs can overcome challenges and create thriving businesses that make a lasting impact.

Resources and Support for Aspiring Entrepreneurs

Aspiring entrepreneurs can access a range of resources and support systems to increase their chances of success. Incubators, accelerators, and coworking spaces provide access to mentorship, funding opportunities, and networking events. Government initiatives and organizations also offer programs and grants to support start-up ventures.

For example, Y Combinator, a renowned start-up accelerator, has helped launch and nurture successful companies such as Airbnb, Dropbox, and Reddit. Through its intensive program, start-ups receive mentorship, funding, and access to a vast network of industry experts and investors.

Entrepreneurship is not without challenges. It requires

resilience, adaptability, and a willingness to learn from failures. However, the rewards can be significant, including financial independence, creative fulfilment, and the ability to make a meaningful impact.

The post-pandemic era offers unique opportunities for entrepreneurship as society transforms various industries. Emerging trends such as remote work, digitalization, and sustainability present fertile ground for innovative start-ups. Entrepreneurs who can identify and address evolving needs and embrace emerging technologies are well-positioned to thrive.

In addition to incubators and accelerators, aspiring entrepreneurs can access various resources and support systems. Business development centres, industry-specific associations, and entrepreneurship networks provide guidance, workshops, and access to experts who can help navigate the complexities of starting a business.

Government initiatives play a crucial role in fostering entrepreneurship. They offer programs that provide financial support, mentorship, and training to aspiring entrepreneurs. Some governments also provide tax incentives and grants to encourage the establishment and growth of start-ups.

Moreover, crowdfunding platforms and angel investor networks offer alternative funding options for entrepreneurs. These platforms connect start-ups with potential investors who believe in their ideas and provide the necessary capital to bring them to fruition.

In conclusion, aspiring entrepreneurs have a wealth of resources and support systems available to them. By leveraging incubators, accelerators, government programs, and networking opportunities, individuals can gain valuable knowledge, access funding, and receive mentorship to navigate the entrepreneurial journey. With the right support, a solid business plan, and a passion for innovation, aspiring entrepreneurs can turn their ideas into successful ventures that contribute to economic growth and societal impact.

CHAPTER IX. EMOTIONAL INTELLIGENCE AND WELL-BEING AT WORK

Importance of Emotional Intelligence in the Workplace

In the post-pandemic job market, emotional intelligence has become a critical skill for success. Emotional intelligence refers to the ability to recognize and manage emotions, both in oneself and in others. It involves skills such as self-awareness, empathy, communication, and relationship management. Emotionally intelligent individuals are better equipped to navigate interpersonal dynamics, resolve conflicts, and build strong professional relationships.

Google, known for its focus on employee well-being, conducted a study called "Project Oxygen" to identify the qualities of its top-performing managers. The study revealed that emotional intelligence, specifically traits like empathy and effective communication, played a significant role in managerial success.

Emotional intelligence enhances teamwork and collaboration. Individuals with high emotional intelligence can understand and respond to the emotions and needs of their colleagues, creating a positive and supportive work environment. This fosters trust, enhances communication, and promotes a sense of belonging among team members.

Emotionally intelligent leaders are adept at managing and resolving conflicts. They can navigate difficult conversations with empathy and find mutually beneficial solutions. By addressing conflicts promptly and constructively, they prevent issues from escalating and maintain a harmonious work environment.

Moreover, emotional intelligence is essential for effective leadership. Leaders who possess emotional intelligence can inspire and motivate their teams, build strong relationships with stakeholders, and navigate organizational challenges with empathy and resilience. They can adapt their leadership style to suit the needs of their team members, resulting in increased employee engagement and productivity.

In conclusion, emotional intelligence is a crucial skill in the workplace. It enhances communication, collaboration, and conflict resolution, and it plays a significant role in effective leadership. Developing emotional intelligence is an ongoing process that involves self-reflection, empathy, and continuous learning. By prioritizing emotional intelligence, individuals can thrive in the post-pandemic job market and contribute to a positive and supportive work environment.

Strategies for Managing Stress and Promoting Mental Well-being

The post-pandemic job market brings with it new challenges and increased stress levels. Individuals must prioritize their mental well-being to maintain productivity and job satisfaction. Strategies for managing stress include practising self-care, setting boundaries, maintaining work-life balance, and seeking support from colleagues and professionals when needed. Mindfulness techniques, such as meditation and breathing exercises, can also help manage stress and enhance well-being.

Companies like LinkedIn have implemented initiatives to promote employee well-being, such as offering mental health resources, organizing wellness challenges, and providing flexible work arrangements. These efforts contribute to a positive work environment and support employees in managing their mental health.

Self-care is an essential strategy for managing stress. This involves taking time for activities that recharge and rejuvenate, such as exercising, spending time in nature, pursuing hobbies, and engaging in relaxation techniques. Setting boundaries is equally important, including defining clear work hours, taking regular breaks, and disconnecting from work-related tasks during non-work hours. By establishing boundaries, individuals can maintain a healthy work-life balance and prevent burnout.

Seeking support from colleagues and professionals is also crucial. Connecting with others who understand the challenges of the job market can provide validation and guidance. It is important to foster open and supportive relationships, where individuals can discuss their concerns and seek advice when needed. Additionally, seeking professional support from therapists or counsellors can offer valuable insights and coping strategies for managing stress and promoting mental well-being.

Mindfulness techniques, such as meditation, deep breathing exercises, and mindfulness-based stress reduction, can be powerful tools for managing stress. These practices cultivate a sense of present-moment awareness, allowing individuals to reduce anxiety, increase resilience, and improve overall well-being. Taking a few minutes each day to engage in these practices can have a significant positive impact on mental health.

In conclusion, managing stress and promoting mental well-being is essential in the post-pandemic job market. By practising self-care, setting boundaries, seeking support, and incorporating mindfulness techniques, individuals can effectively manage stress, enhance well-being, and thrive in their professional endeavours. Employers also play a critical role in creating a supportive work environment by providing resources, fostering open communication, and promoting a culture of well-being. Prioritizing mental health is key to achieving personal and professional success in the post-pandemic job market.

Creating a Supportive and Inclusive Work Environment

A supportive and inclusive work environment is essential for employee engagement and productivity. Employers should foster a culture that values diversity, promotes psychological safety, and encourages open communication. By embracing diversity and creating inclusive practices, organizations can tap into the diverse perspectives and talents of their workforce.

Salesforce, a leading technology company, prioritizes inclusivity and has implemented programs like "Equality Groups" to support underrepresented employees. These groups provide a platform for networking, mentorship, and professional development, contributing to an inclusive work environment.

Emotional intelligence and well-being not only benefit individuals but also contribute to the overall success of organizations. Companies that prioritize employee well-being and create a supportive work environment are more likely to attract and retain top talent, enhance team collaboration, and drive innovation.

In conclusion, emotional intelligence and well-being are crucial elements in navigating the post-pandemic job market successfully. By developing emotional intelligence skills, individuals can effectively manage relationships, resolve conflicts, and thrive in diverse workplace settings. Prioritizing mental well-being and creating a supportive work environment is key to fostering employee engagement and productivity. Employers and employees alike should invest in developing emotional intelligence and implementing strategies to promote well-being to create a positive and thriving work culture.

CHAPTER X. DIVERSITY AND INCLUSION IN THE WORKPLACE

Understanding the Value of Diversity and Inclusion

In the post-pandemic job market, organizations recognize that diversity and inclusion are not just buzzwords, but essential components for success. Diversity encompasses differences in race, gender, age, ethnicity, sexual orientation, abilities, and more. Inclusion, on the other hand, refers to creating an environment where every individual feels valued, respected, and supported. Embracing diversity and fostering inclusion brings numerous benefits, including enhanced innovation, improved decision-making, and increased employee satisfaction.

The tech giant Microsoft has implemented diversity and inclusion initiatives, such as setting goals for diverse hiring and requiring diverse interview panels. These efforts have resulted in a more inclusive work environment and a diverse talent pool.

Diversity brings fresh perspectives and experiences to the table, leading to more innovative and creative solutions. When teams are composed of individuals with different backgrounds and perspectives, they are better equipped to understand the needs of diverse customer bases and create products and services that cater to a wide range of users.

Inclusive environments promote collaboration and open communication, enabling employees to freely express their ideas and opinions. This leads to improved decision-making processes, as diverse perspectives challenge assumptions and encourage critical thinking. Inclusive workplaces also foster a sense of belonging, allowing employees to bring their whole selves to work and feel valued for their unique contributions.

Furthermore, organizations that prioritize diversity and inclusion are more likely to attract and retain top talent. In a competitive job market, job seekers actively seek out companies that prioritize diversity and create inclusive cultures. Employees who feel included and valued are more engaged, motivated, and committed to their work.

In conclusion, understanding the value of diversity and inclusion is crucial in the post-pandemic job market. Embracing diversity and fostering inclusion not only brings numerous benefits to organizations, such as increased innovation and improved decision-making but also helps attract and retain top talent. By creating a culture that values and embraces diversity, organizations can create a positive and inclusive work environment that sets them apart in the job market.

Overcoming Biases and Promoting Inclusivity

Unconscious biases can hinder diversity and inclusion efforts in the workplace. Recognizing and challenging these biases is crucial for creating a fair and equitable work environment. Organizations can implement training programs and policies that address biases, promote awareness, and encourage inclusive behaviours. By fostering a culture that values diverse perspectives and experiences, individuals can overcome biases and contribute to a more inclusive workplace.

Accenture, a global professional services company, introduced the "Getting to Equal" program, which includes unconscious bias training and encourages employees to actively challenge their biases. The program has resulted in increased gender diversity and inclusion within the company.

Overcoming biases starts with self-awareness. Individuals should reflect on their own biases and assumptions, challenging them to see beyond stereotypes and preconceived notions. By recognizing the impact of biases on decision-making and interactions, individuals can consciously make efforts to be more inclusive and open-minded.

Organizations play a vital role in promoting inclusivity by implementing policies and practices that foster an inclusive environment. This includes diverse hiring practices, equitable promotion, and advancement opportunities, and creating spaces for open dialogue and collaboration. By providing unconscious bias training and educational resources, organizations can empower employees to actively challenge biases and create a culture of inclusivity.

Leaders within organizations also have a responsibility to model inclusive behaviours and champion diversity. By setting an example and emphasizing the importance of diversity and inclusion, leaders can create a supportive environment that values different perspectives and experiences. This can be achieved through diverse leadership teams, inclusive decision-making processes, and fostering an environment where employees feel safe to share their opinions.

In conclusion, overcoming biases and promoting inclusivity is a crucial endeavour in the post-pandemic job market. Organizations can implement training programs, policies, and practices that address biases and create an inclusive workplace. Individuals can play their part by challenging their own biases, being open-minded, and actively contributing to a culture of inclusivity. By collectively working towards inclusivity, we can create workplaces that embrace diversity and unlock the full potential of all individuals.

Strategies for Fostering a Diverse and Inclusive Work Culture

Creating a diverse and inclusive work culture requires ongoing commitment and intentional actions. Some strategies include implementing inclusive hiring practices, providing equal opportunities for growth and advancement, fostering inclusive leadership, and establishing employee resource groups. Organizations should also prioritize the development of policies that support work-life balance and flexibility, accommodating diverse needs and promoting inclusivity.

Salesforce, a leading CRM company, has a dedicated Chief Equality Officer responsible for driving diversity and inclusion initiatives. The company has established employee resource groups focused on various dimensions of diversity, such as race, gender, and LGBTQ+ issues, to provide support and create an inclusive workplace.

By embracing diversity and fostering inclusion, organizations can tap into a wide range of perspectives, ideas, and experiences, leading to greater innovation, improved decision-making, and a stronger bottom line. Creating a diverse and inclusive work culture requires ongoing commitment, education, and the active involvement of all employees.

Implementing inclusive hiring practices is a crucial step towards building a diverse workforce. This includes using diverse sourcing channels, ensuring diverse interview panels, and providing unconscious bias training for hiring managers. By actively seeking candidates from different backgrounds and perspectives, organizations can create a more inclusive talent pool.

Equal opportunities for growth and advancement are essential for fostering a diverse and inclusive work culture. Organizations should provide mentorship programs, and leadership development initiatives, and establish clear pathways for career progression. By providing equal access to opportunities and recognizing diverse talents, organizations can nurture an inclusive environment that values everyone's contributions.

Inclusive leadership is another critical aspect of fostering a diverse and inclusive work culture. Leaders should actively promote diversity, champion inclusive practices, and create a psychologically safe environment where all employees feel valued and heard. By modelling inclusive behaviours and actively seeking input from diverse team members, leaders can set the tone for an inclusive workplace.

Establishing employee resource groups (ERGs) can provide a platform for employees to connect, share experiences, and drive initiatives that promote diversity and inclusion. ERGs focused on various dimensions of diversity can offer support, networking opportunities, and educational resources. These groups can play a vital role in fostering a sense of belonging and driving positive change within the organization.

In conclusion, fostering a diverse and inclusive work culture is a key priority in the post-pandemic job market. Organizations that prioritize diversity and inclusion create a work environment that celebrates differences and fosters collaboration. Overcoming biases and promoting inclusivity requires ongoing efforts, including training programs, inclusive policies, and supportive leadership. By embracing diversity and fostering inclusion, organizations can unlock the full potential of their workforce and drive sustainable success in the evolving world of work.

CHAPTER XI. REMOTE LEADERSHIP AND TEAM MANAGEMENT

Effective Leadership in a Remote Work Environment

Leading remote teams requires a different approach compared to traditional in-person leadership. Remote leaders must possess strong communication skills, adaptability, and empathy. They need to set clear expectations, provide guidance, and foster a sense of trust among team members. Effective remote leaders leverage technology to facilitate seamless communication and collaboration while also prioritizing employee well-being and work-life balance.

Buffer, a fully remote company, emphasizes transparency and asynchronous communication. Their leaders use video calls, team chat platforms, and project management tools to stay connected with their remote team members and ensure efficient collaboration.

Communication is a fundamental aspect of effective remote leadership. Remote leaders need to establish regular check-ins, encourage open dialogue, and use various communication channels to facilitate team collaboration. They must be clear and concise in their communication, ensuring that expectations, goals, and deadlines are effectively conveyed. Additionally, remote leaders should actively listen to their team members, provide timely feedback, and address any concerns or challenges that may arise.

Adaptability is another crucial quality for remote leaders. They need to be flexible and adaptable in the face of changing circumstances. Remote work environments can bring unique challenges, such as different time zones, cultural differences, and varying levels of technology proficiency. Effective leaders can adjust their leadership style to accommodate these differences and find innovative solutions to overcome obstacles.

Empathy plays a significant role in remote leadership. Remote leaders should strive to understand the unique needs and challenges of their team members, considering the diverse range of home environments, personal circumstances, and potential feelings of isolation. By demonstrating empathy, leaders can build trust, foster a positive team culture, and support the overall well-being of their remote employees.

Technology is a vital tool for effective remote leadership. Remote leaders should be proficient in using communication and collaboration tools, project management software, and other digital platforms. They need to ensure that their team members have access to the necessary tools and resources to work efficiently from remote locations. Additionally, remote leaders should be knowledgeable about cybersecurity measures to protect sensitive information and ensure data privacy.

In conclusion, effective leadership in a remote work environment requires strong communication skills, adaptability, empathy, and leveraging technology to facilitate seamless collaboration. Remote leaders must establish clear expectations, provide guidance, and prioritize employee well-being. By embracing these qualities and strategies, leaders can effectively lead remote teams, drive productivity, and foster a positive work culture in the post-pandemic job market.

Strategies for Managing Remote Teams and Fostering Collaboration

Managing remote teams involves overcoming geographical barriers and facilitating collaboration in a virtual environment. Remote team managers can implement strategies such as regular check-ins, goal setting, and establishing virtual team-building activities. They can also leverage collaboration tools, project management software, and cloud-based platforms to enhance productivity and keep everyone aligned.

Automatic, the company behind WordPress, has a distributed workforce with employees working from different locations worldwide. To foster collaboration, they use tools like Slack and Zoom for real-time communication while also organizing annual company-wide meetups to strengthen relationships among team members.

Regular check-ins are essential for managing remote teams effectively. Managers should schedule one-on-one meetings or team meetings to discuss progress, address concerns, and provide guidance. These check-ins help keep everyone aligned, build rapport, and ensure that team members feel supported and connected.

Goal setting is crucial for remote teams as it provides clarity and direction. Managers should establish clear goals, communicate expectations, and track progress regularly. Setting SMART (Specific, Measurable, Achievable, Relevant, Time-bound) goals help team members stay focused and motivated while providing a sense of accomplishment and accountability.

Virtual team-building activities are essential for fostering collaboration and building relationships among remote team members. Managers can organize virtual coffee breaks, team-building games, or even virtual social events to create a sense of camaraderie and promote team cohesion. These activities help bridge the distance and cultivate a positive team culture.

Leveraging collaboration tools and project management software is essential for remote teams to work efficiently. Platforms like Slack, Microsoft Teams, or Google Workspace enable real-time communication, file sharing, and collaboration on projects. Project management tools such as Asana, Trello, or Jira help track tasks, assign responsibilities, and monitor progress. Cloud-based platforms allow team members to access and collaborate on documents and files from anywhere, ensuring seamless collaboration.

Effective communication is key to managing remote teams and fostering collaboration. Managers should encourage open and transparent communication, set clear expectations, and provide timely feedback. They should create channels for team members to share ideas, ask questions, and provide updates. Additionally, using video conferencing instead of relying solely on written communication can enhance understanding and build stronger connections among team members.

In conclusion, managing remote teams and fostering collaboration requires implementing strategies such as regular check-ins, goal setting, and virtual team-building activities. Leveraging collaboration tools and effective communication practices are also crucial. By embracing these strategies, managers can effectively manage remote teams, enhance productivity, and create a collaborative and connected virtual work environment in the post-pandemic job market.

Building Trust and Maintaining Employee Engagement in a Virtual Setting

Building trust and maintaining employee engagement is crucial for remote teams. Leaders can build trust by being transparent, responsive, and supportive. Regular communication, both one-on-one and in team meetings, helps foster a sense of belonging and keeps employees engaged. Encouraging social interaction and virtual team-building activities can also help strengthen relationships and maintain team morale.

GitLab, a remote company specializing in software development, encourages virtual coffee chats, team-building exercises, and non-work-related discussions through dedicated Slack channels. These initiatives help build rapport and maintain a strong sense of community among remote team members.

In a post-pandemic job market where, remote work is increasingly prevalent, effective remote leadership and team management skills are essential. Leaders who adapt to remote work dynamics and prioritize effective communication, collaboration, and employee well-being will succeed in leading high-performing remote teams.

Transparency is key to building trust in a virtual setting. Leaders should share information about the company's goals, decisions, and progress. By keeping employees informed, they foster a sense of inclusion and trust among team members. Being responsive and accessible to employees' questions, concerns, and feedback is also crucial. Promptly addressing issues and providing support when needed demonstrates a commitment to employee well-being and shows that their voices are valued.

Regular communication is essential for maintaining employee engagement. Leaders should schedule regular check-ins, team meetings, and virtual town halls to keep everyone connected and informed. These communication channels provide opportunities for clarifying expectations, sharing updates, and celebrating achievements. One-on-one meetings are particularly important for building individual connections, discussing professional growth, and providing personalized support.

Encouraging social interaction and virtual team-building activities is vital for maintaining team morale and strengthening relationships. Leaders can organize virtual social events, team challenges, or informal chats to foster a sense of camaraderie and create opportunities for team members to connect on a personal level. By fostering a positive and supportive team culture, leaders promote engagement and collaboration.

In conclusion, remote leadership and team management require a unique set of skills and strategies. Effective leaders in remote work environments prioritize communication, foster collaboration, and build trust among team members. By leveraging technology, setting clear expectations, and supporting employee engagement, leaders can ensure the success and productivity of their remote teams. Embracing remote work and mastering remote leadership skills are key to navigating the post-pandemic job market and thriving in the evolving world of work.

CHAPTER XII.
THE FUTURE OF TRADITIONAL INDUSTRIES

The Impact of Technology on Traditional Industries

The advent of technology has significantly impacted traditional industries across various sectors. Automation, artificial intelligence, and digitization have disrupted traditional business models and workflows. Industries such as manufacturing, retail, and transportation have witnessed significant changes in operations and customer interactions. Technology has enabled greater efficiency, streamlined processes, and enhanced customer experiences in these industries.

The automotive industry has experienced the integration of technology with the rise of electric vehicles and autonomous driving. Electric vehicles have disrupted the traditional combustion engine market, leading to a shift in production and supply chains. Autonomous driving technology is transforming transportation and logistics, promising safer and more efficient mobility solutions.

Retail is another industry greatly impacted by technology. E-commerce platforms have revolutionized the way consumers shop, offering convenience, a wide range of products, and personalized recommendations. Brick-and-mortar retailers have had to adapt by integrating online channels and enhancing in-store experiences with technologies like augmented reality and contactless payments. Furthermore, advanced data analytics enable retailers to understand consumer behaviour and preferences, enabling targeted marketing campaigns and personalized shopping experiences.

The manufacturing sector has seen significant changes through the adoption of automation and robotics. Smart factories equipped with connected machines and IoT sensors enable real-time monitoring and optimization of production processes. Robotics and AI have automated repetitive tasks, increasing efficiency, reducing errors, and improving overall productivity. These advancements have reshaped the manufacturing landscape, making it more agile and responsive to customer demands.

The impact of technology is not limited to specific industries but extends to various aspects of business operations. Cloud computing has revolutionized data storage and access, enabling remote collaboration and scalability. Advanced analytics and big data allow businesses to gain valuable insights, make data-driven decisions, and identify market trends. Communication technologies, such as video conferencing and instant messaging, have transformed the way teams collaborate, enabling remote work and global connectivity.

However, the impact of technology on traditional industries is not without challenges. Workforce displacement and job transformation are concerns as automation replaces certain tasks. Businesses also face cybersecurity risks and ethical considerations surrounding data privacy and AI algorithms. It is crucial for organizations to proactively address these challenges through reskilling programs, strong cybersecurity measures, and responsible technology practices.

In conclusion, technology has had a profound impact on traditional industries, reshaping operations, and customer experiences. Embracing technology is essential for businesses to stay competitive and thrive in the evolving marketplace. Adapting to technological advancements, leveraging data and analytics, and fostering a culture of innovation are key to successfully navigating the impact of technology on traditional industries.

Opportunities for Innovation and Transformation

Despite the challenges posed by technology, traditional industries also present opportunities for innovation and transformation. Embracing new technologies and leveraging data analytics can lead to enhanced product offerings, improved operational efficiency, and better customer insights. Companies that proactively embrace innovation can gain a competitive edge and secure their position in the post-pandemic job market.

The healthcare industry is transforming through the adoption of telemedicine and digital health solutions. Remote consultations, wearable devices, and health monitoring apps have revolutionized patient care and made healthcare services more accessible. This innovation has opened new avenues for healthcare professionals and created job opportunities in the digital health sector.

The energy sector is another traditional industry that is ripe for innovation. The increasing demand for renewable energy sources and the push towards sustainability have led to advancements in solar and wind technologies. Energy storage solutions, such as battery technology, are paving the way for more reliable and efficient power systems. Innovations in the energy sector not only contribute to environmental conservation but also create opportunities for new jobs and economic growth.

The construction industry is embracing technological advancements such as Building Information Modelling (BIM), augmented reality, and robotics. These technologies streamline construction processes, enhance project coordination, and improve worker safety. Prefabrication and modular construction methods are reducing construction timelines and costs. The integration of IoT sensors and smart systems in buildings enables efficient energy management and maintenance. Innovations in the construction industry have the potential to transform the way buildings are designed, constructed, and operated.

Furthermore, traditional industries can leverage data analytics and AI to gain valuable insights, optimize processes, and personalize customer experiences. Retailers can use data to forecast demand, tailor marketing campaigns, and optimize inventory management. Manufacturers can implement predictive maintenance to minimize downtime and improve productivity. Financial institutions can leverage AI for fraud detection and risk assessment. These advancements not only enhance efficiency but also create new job opportunities in data analysis and AI implementation.

In conclusion, traditional industries present ample opportunities for innovation and transformation. Embracing new technologies, leveraging data analytics, and fostering a culture of innovation can lead to improved products, streamlined operations, and enhanced customer experiences. Companies that proactively seek out and embrace these opportunities can position themselves for success in the post-pandemic job market. By embracing innovation, traditional industries can not only adapt to the changing landscape but also contribute to economic growth and societal advancement.

**Adapting to Changing Consumer Behaviours and Market

Demands**

Traditional industries must adapt to changing consumer behaviours and market demands to remain relevant. Understanding customer preferences, embracing e-commerce, and leveraging data-driven insights are essential for staying competitive. Companies need to invest in digital marketing, personalized customer experiences, and agile supply chain management to meet evolving customer expectations.

The retail industry has experienced a shift towards e-commerce and omnichannel strategies. Traditional brick-and-mortar stores have embraced online platforms, allowing customers to shop from anywhere at any time. Retailers that have successfully adapted to this change have witnessed growth and expanded their customer base. They have implemented personalized marketing campaigns, leveraged social media platforms, and utilized customer data to deliver tailored shopping experiences.

In the food and beverage industry, changing consumer preferences and a growing focus on health and sustainability have prompted companies to introduce plant-based alternatives and eco-friendly packaging. Food delivery services have also seen a surge in demand, leading to the rise of ghost kitchens and delivery-only establishments. Adapting to these market demands requires agility in operations, menu offerings, and marketing strategies.

The hospitality and tourism industry has faced significant challenges due to travel restrictions and changing consumer behaviours. To adapt, hotels and resorts have implemented rigorous health and safety protocols, introduced contactless check-ins, and enhanced their digital presence to attract local customers. Travel agencies have shifted their focus to domestic travel and customized experiences to meet the preferences of cautious travellers.

The entertainment industry has witnessed a shift towards digital platforms as consumers increasingly seek entertainment options from the comfort of their homes. Streaming services, online gaming, and virtual events have gained popularity. Traditional media companies have embraced digital platforms to distribute content, while live event organizers have explored virtual formats to engage audiences.

In conclusion, traditional industries face both challenges and opportunities in the post-pandemic job market. The impact of technology and changing consumer behaviours require businesses to innovate and transform their operations. Embracing new technologies, understanding customer needs, and adapting to market demands are crucial for success. By recognizing the innovation potential and actively seeking ways to evolve, traditional industries can thrive and create new job opportunities in the changing landscape of work.

CHAPTER XIII. THE RISE OF SUSTAINABLE AND ETHICAL BUSINESS PRACTICES

The Importance of Sustainability and Corporate Social Responsibility

In the post-pandemic job market, there is an increasing emphasis on sustainability and corporate social responsibility (CSR). Businesses are realizing the importance of operating in an environmentally and socially responsible manner. Sustainability practices not only contribute to environmental conservation but also enhance a company's reputation and attract socially conscious consumers and employees. Adopting sustainable practices can lead to cost savings, resource efficiency, and long-term business resilience.

Patagonia, an outdoor clothing, and gear company is renowned for its commitment to environmental sustainability. The company has implemented initiatives such as using recycled materials, promoting fair labour practices, and donating a portion of its sales to environmental causes. Patagonia's sustainability efforts have resonated with consumers who prioritize ethical and sustainable products.

Beyond consumer preferences, sustainability and CSR have

become key considerations for employees. Job seekers are increasingly drawn to companies that demonstrate a commitment to social and environmental issues. Employees want to work for organizations that align with their values and contribute to positive change. Companies that prioritize sustainability and CSR initiatives attract and retain top talent, fostering a motivated and engaged workforce.

Furthermore, sustainable practices can drive innovation and business growth. Companies that invest in sustainable technologies and practices often discover new efficiencies, reduce waste, and optimize resource management. This can lead to cost savings and improved operational performance. Sustainable innovation also opens opportunities for new markets and product development, responding to the growing demand for environmentally friendly solutions.

Corporate social responsibility goes beyond environmental initiatives. It encompasses actions that benefit communities and society at large. This includes philanthropic efforts, volunteer programs, and initiatives to promote diversity, equity, and inclusion within the organization. Embracing CSR can strengthen the company's relationship with stakeholders, including employees, customers, investors, and the wider community.

In conclusion, sustainability and corporate social responsibility are integral components of the post-pandemic job market. Businesses that prioritize sustainability practices and embrace CSR initiatives position themselves for long-term success. By demonstrating a commitment to environmental conservation, social impact, and ethical business practices, companies can attract customers, engage employees, drive innovation, and contribute to a more sustainable and inclusive future.

Integrating Sustainability into Business Strategies

Integrating sustainability into business strategies involves incorporating environmental and social considerations into decision-making processes. This includes setting sustainability goals, implementing environmentally friendly practices, and engaging stakeholders in sustainable initiatives. Sustainable business practices can range from reducing carbon emissions, adopting renewable energy sources, and implementing waste reduction strategies to promoting diversity and inclusion in the workforce.

Unilever, a multinational consumer goods company, has integrated sustainability into its business strategy through its Sustainable Living Plan. The plan focuses on reducing the company's environmental footprint, improving the livelihoods of its workers, and positively impacting society. Unilever's commitment to sustainability has not only led to positive environmental outcomes but has also enhanced its brand reputation and attracted environmentally conscious consumers.

Integrating sustainability into business strategies offers several benefits. First, it enables companies to meet the evolving expectations of consumers and stakeholders. Consumers are increasingly concerned about the environmental and social impact of the products and services they purchase. By integrating sustainability into business strategies, companies can align their offerings with consumer preferences and gain a competitive edge.

Second, sustainability can drive innovation and efficiency. Companies that prioritize sustainability are often motivated to find creative solutions that reduce resource consumption, optimize processes, and minimize waste. This can result in cost savings, improved operational performance, and a more resilient supply chain.

Moreover, sustainability considerations are crucial in risk

management. Businesses face a range of environmental and social risks, such as regulatory changes, reputational damage, and supply chain disruptions. By integrating sustainability into their strategies, companies can identify and address these risks proactively, mitigating potential negative impacts.

To successfully integrate sustainability, businesses must establish clear goals, embed sustainability practices across all levels of the organization, and engage stakeholders. This involves collaboration with suppliers, customers, employees, and local communities to create shared value and drive positive change. Transparent reporting and measurement of sustainability performance are also essential to track progress, demonstrate accountability, and communicate with stakeholders.

In conclusion, integrating sustainability into business strategies is crucial in the post-pandemic job market. Companies that embrace sustainability gain a competitive advantage, drive innovation, and build resilience. By addressing environmental and social challenges, businesses can contribute to a more sustainable future while meeting the expectations of consumers, employees, and other stakeholders.

Consumer Preferences and the Demand for Ethical Products and Services

Consumer preferences are evolving, and there is an increasing demand for ethical and sustainable products and services. Today, consumers consider factors such as the environmental impact, ethical sourcing of materials, and the social responsibility of companies when making purchasing decisions. Businesses that align their offerings with these consumer preferences have a competitive advantage in the post-pandemic job market.

Tesla, an electric vehicle manufacturer, has experienced

significant success due to the growing demand for sustainable transportation. Consumers are increasingly aware of the environmental impact of traditional combustion engine vehicles and are opting for electric vehicles as a greener alternative. Tesla's innovative electric cars have captured a substantial market share and have propelled the company to become a leader in the sustainable transportation industry.

Businesses across various sectors are recognizing the importance of meeting consumer demands for ethical products and services. They are incorporating sustainability and corporate social responsibility (CSR) into their operations, supply chains, and marketing strategies. This includes initiatives such as reducing carbon emissions, sourcing ethically produced materials, supporting fair trade practices, and contributing to social causes.

The demand for ethical products and services is driven by several factors. First, there is an increased awareness of environmental issues such as climate change, deforestation, and pollution. Consumers are actively seeking products and services that have a lower environmental footprint and contribute to a more sustainable future.

Second, there is a growing concern for social justice and fair labour practices. Consumers are interested in knowing that the products they purchase are made under fair working conditions and that workers are paid fair wages. They also appreciate companies that prioritize diversity and inclusion in their workforce and support local communities.

Furthermore, technological advancements and increased access to information have empowered consumers to make more informed choices. They can easily research and compare products, read reviews, and assess a company's sustainability and social responsibility practices. Businesses that fail to meet these expectations risk losing customers and damaging their reputation.

In conclusion, the rise of sustainable and ethical business practices is transforming the post-pandemic job market. Consumers are demanding products and services that align with their values and have a positive impact on the environment and society. Businesses that prioritize sustainability and corporate social responsibility gain a competitive edge, attract loyal customers, and position themselves as leaders in their industries. As the demand for ethical products and services continues to grow, businesses that embrace sustainability will be well-positioned for success in the evolving work landscape.

CHAPTER XIV.
FUTURE SKILLS
FOR EMERGING
TECHNOLOGIES

Exploring Emerging Technologies and Their Impact on Jobs

In the post-pandemic job market, emerging technologies are reshaping the future of work. Artificial intelligence (AI), blockchain, cybersecurity, and other technologies are revolutionizing industries and creating new job opportunities. Individuals must understand these technologies and their implications to stay relevant in the evolving job market.

The adoption of AI-powered chatbots in customer service has streamlined interactions and improved efficiency. Companies like Amazon and Apple have integrated chatbots into their customer support systems, reducing the need for human agents in handling routine inquiries. While this may lead to a decrease in certain job roles, it also opens opportunities in designing, programming, and maintaining these AI systems.

Blockchain technology, known for its decentralized and secure nature, has disrupted various industries such as finance, supply chain management, and healthcare. Its potential applications range from digital currencies and smart contracts to transparent supply chain tracking and secure medical records.

As blockchain adoption increases, there will be a demand for professionals skilled in blockchain development, cybersecurity, and data analysis.

Cybersecurity has become a critical concern as businesses increasingly rely on digital infrastructure. The rise of remote work and cloud computing has heightened the need for robust cybersecurity measures to protect sensitive data and prevent cyber threats. As a result, the demand for cybersecurity specialists, ethical hackers, and data privacy experts has significantly increased.

Moreover, the Internet of Things (IoT) has connected various devices, enabling the exchange of data and automation of processes. IoT technology has applications in smart homes, healthcare monitoring, and industrial automation. Professionals with expertise in IoT architecture, data analytics, and cybersecurity will be in high demand to ensure the seamless integration and security of IoT devices.

While emerging technologies may automate certain tasks and job functions, they also create new job opportunities. Individuals need to embrace lifelong learning and acquire skills that complement these technologies. Upskilling in areas such as data science, AI programming, cybersecurity, and blockchain development can help individuals adapt and thrive in the changing job market.

In conclusion, emerging technologies are reshaping the job market, creating new opportunities, and transforming existing roles. Individuals need to stay informed about these technologies, understand their implications, and acquire the necessary skills to remain competitive. Embracing lifelong learning and adapting to technological advancements will be key to success in the post-pandemic job market.

IBM's Watson, an AI-powered system, is used in various industries, including healthcare, finance, and cybersecurity. Professionals with the skills to develop and deploy AI solutions like Watson are in high demand as organizations seek to leverage AI capabilities.

C. Navigating the intersection of technology and humanity.
As technology advances, the human element becomes increasingly important. The ability to navigate the intersection of technology and humanity is critical for success in the post-pandemic job market. Skills such as critical thinking, creativity, emotional intelligence, and adaptability are essential for individuals to work collaboratively with technology and leverage its benefits.

In the healthcare sector, the integration of technology and humanity is evident in telemedicine. Healthcare professionals need to leverage digital tools to deliver remote care effectively while maintaining empathy and understanding of their patient's needs.

In conclusion, the future of work is closely intertwined with emerging technologies. Individuals who develop skills in areas such as artificial intelligence, blockchain, and cybersecurity will be well-positioned for the jobs of tomorrow. However, it is equally important to recognize the significance of human skills and qualities in navigating the intersection of technology and humanity. By embracing both technical and soft skills, individuals can adapt to the changing landscape and thrive in the post-pandemic job market.

CHAPTER XV. WORKFORCE DIVERSITY AND AGE INCLUSIVITY

Challenges and Opportunities of Age Diversity in the Workplace

In the post-pandemic job market, age diversity in the workplace brings both challenges and opportunities. While it can create generational gaps and differences, it also presents an opportunity for innovation, collaboration, and knowledge exchange across different generations.

One of the challenges of age diversity is the potential for generational gaps. Different generations may have varying communication styles, work preferences, and technological skills. This can lead to miscommunication, misunderstandings, and difficulty in working together effectively. Bridging these gaps requires open-mindedness, empathy, and a willingness to learn from one another.

However, age diversity also brings a wealth of opportunities. Each generation brings unique perspectives, experiences, and skills to the table. Older employees often have a wealth of industry knowledge and expertise, while younger employees may possess fresh ideas, technological savvy, and a drive for innovation. By fostering collaboration and creating a culture of inclusivity, organizations can harness the collective strengths of different generations to drive creativity, problem-solving, and overall business success.

IBM is an example of a company that recognizes and promotes age diversity in the workplace. They have implemented programs that encourage older employees to mentor and share their knowledge with younger colleagues. This intergenerational collaboration not only facilitates the transfer of valuable expertise but also fosters a culture of innovation and learning. By leveraging the strengths of each generation, IBM has created a dynamic work environment that benefits employees and the company.

To fully embrace the opportunities of age diversity, organizations should provide training and development programs that cater to the needs and aspirations of employees of all age groups. This can include mentorship programs, reverse mentoring initiatives, and cross-generational team projects. Additionally, promoting an inclusive and respectful work culture that values the contributions of individuals regardless of their age fosters a positive environment where all employees can thrive.

In conclusion, age diversity in the workplace presents both challenges and opportunities. By embracing the unique perspectives and skills of different generations, organizations can foster innovation, collaboration, and continuous learning. Through intergenerational collaboration and inclusive practices, organizations can leverage the strengths of each generation and create a harmonious and productive work environment in the post-pandemic job market.

Promoting Age Inclusivity and Combating Ageism

Promoting age inclusivity in the workplace is essential to create a diverse and thriving workforce. Ageism, discrimination, or prejudice based on a person's age, can limit opportunities, and hinder professional growth. To combat ageism, organizations must address age-related biases and create an inclusive work environment that values the contributions of individuals of all ages.

One-way organizations can promote age inclusivity is by implementing fair hiring practices. This includes eliminating age-related biases in recruitment and selection processes, ensuring equal opportunities for candidates of all ages, and focusing on skills and qualifications rather than age. Emphasizing the importance of diverse perspectives and experiences during hiring decisions can help combat ageism.

Furthermore, providing training and development opportunities for employees at all stages of their careers is crucial. This includes offering lifelong learning programs, mentorship initiatives, and skill-building workshops that cater to employees of different age groups. By investing in the professional growth and development of older workers, organizations can harness their expertise and ensure their continued engagement and contribution.

Creating an inclusive work environment is also vital. Organizations should foster a culture that values and respects individuals of all ages. This can be achieved by promoting intergenerational collaboration, encouraging knowledge-sharing, and recognizing the unique strengths and perspectives that employees of different age groups bring to the table. Emphasizing teamwork, open communication, and mutual respect can help break down age-related barriers and foster a sense of belonging for all employees.

The AARP (American Association of Retired Persons) Foundation is an example of an organization actively advocating for age inclusivity in the workplace. They provide resources, tools, and support to both employees and employers to combat ageism and promote a diverse and inclusive workforce. Their initiatives aim to raise awareness about age-related biases and challenge stereotypes surrounding older workers.

In conclusion, promoting age inclusivity and combating ageism is essential for creating an inclusive and equitable work environment. By implementing fair hiring practices, providing development opportunities, and fostering an inclusive culture, organizations can harness the full potential of a diverse workforce. Embracing age diversity contributes to innovation, enhances productivity, and ensures that individuals of all ages can thrive in the post-pandemic job market.

Leveraging the Experience and Skills of Multi-generational Teams

Multi-generational teams bring together individuals from different age groups, each with their own unique experiences, perspectives, and skills. Organizations that leverage the diversity of these teams can benefit from increased innovation, creativity, and problem-solving capabilities. By fostering an inclusive environment that encourages collaboration and mutual respect, teams can effectively leverage the strengths of different generations.

At General Electric (GE), the "GE Global New Directions" program exemplifies the utilization of multi-generational teams. This program specifically focuses on bringing together employees from different generations to work on innovative projects. By combining the diverse experiences and perspectives of employees, GE promotes collaboration and harnesses the collective wisdom of its multi-generational workforce.

The advantages of multi-generational teams lie in their ability to bring a wide range of skills and knowledge to the table. Younger employees often possess fresh perspectives, technological proficiency, and a familiarity with emerging trends. On the other hand, older employees bring extensive experience, institutional knowledge, and a wealth of industry expertise. By fostering an environment where individuals of all ages feel valued and respected, organizations can encourage knowledge-sharing and collaboration among team members.

To leverage the experience and skills of multi-generational teams, organizations should promote intergenerational mentorship and reverse mentorship programs. This enables the transfer of knowledge and skills between generations, allowing individuals to learn from one another and bridge any potential generation gaps. By creating opportunities for open dialogue and mutual learning, organizations can tap into collective expertise and maximize the potential of multi-generational teams.

In conclusion, embracing age diversity and fostering age inclusivity in the workplace is crucial for organizations to thrive in the post-pandemic job market. Multi-generational teams offer a wealth of skills, experiences, and perspectives that, when leveraged effectively, can drive innovation and success. By creating an inclusive environment that encourages collaboration and knowledge-sharing, organizations can harness the collective power of multi-generational teams and excel in the evolving world of work.

CHAPTER XVI.
REMOTE LEARNING
AND EDUCATION

Transformations in Education and Remote Learning

The post-pandemic job market has brought about a rapid transformation in the field of education, with a significant shift towards remote learning. Educational institutions and professionals have quickly adapted to new teaching and learning methodologies, leveraging digital tools and platforms to facilitate online education. This transformation has not only ensured the continuity of education during challenging times but has also opened new opportunities for individuals to gain knowledge and skills from the comfort of their own homes.

Online learning platforms like Coursera have witnessed a surge in enrolment during the pandemic as people have sought to upskill and reskill. These platforms offer a wide range of courses from top universities and institutions, providing individuals with flexible learning options. Through remote learning, individuals can access educational resources and acquire new skills that are relevant to the evolving job market.

The transformations in education and remote learning have several benefits. Firstly, remote learning provides individuals with the flexibility to learn at their own pace and on their schedule, removing geographical barriers and allowing access to a diverse range of courses and programs. Secondly, it fosters self-discipline and self-motivation as individuals take ownership of their learning journey. Remote learning also encourages the development of digital literacy skills, which are increasingly essential in today's digital-driven work environment.

Furthermore, remote learning has opened new possibilities for collaboration and networking. Virtual classrooms and discussion forums enable learners to connect with peers and experts from around the world, facilitating knowledge sharing and the exchange of ideas. Remote learning also encourages individuals to develop essential skills such as time management, self-directed learning, and adaptability - skills that are highly valued in the post-pandemic job market.

In conclusion, the transformations in education and the rise of remote learning have had a profound impact on the post-pandemic job market. Individuals now have access to a wealth of educational resources and can acquire new skills from the comfort of their own homes. The flexibility, accessibility, and opportunities for collaboration offered by remote learning have made it an essential component of the evolving educational landscape. As individuals embrace remote learning, they are better equipped to navigate the changing job market and seize new opportunities for growth and success.

The Future of Online Education and E-Learning Platforms

The future of education is being shaped by the integration of online learning and e-learning platforms. These platforms have revolutionized the way individuals acquire knowledge and skills, providing accessible and flexible learning opportunities that transcend geographical boundaries. As technology continues to advance, the future of online education holds even greater potential for immersive and interactive learning experiences.

E-learning platforms like Udacity are leading the way in this transformative landscape. Udacity offers nano degree programs in collaboration with industry leaders, focusing on practical skills that are in high demand in the job market. Learners can work on real-world projects, gaining hands-on experience that prepares them for the challenges of their chosen field. This industry-driven approach ensures that learners acquire relevant skills and knowledge that directly translate into career opportunities.

The future of online education will see a continued emphasis on personalized learning experiences. Adaptive learning technologies will enable platforms to tailor educational content to individual learners, ensuring that they receive the right level of challenge and support. Additionally, the integration of virtual reality (VR) and augmented reality (AR) will create immersive learning environments, allowing learners to engage with content more interactively and dynamically.

Furthermore, online education will continue to foster collaboration and networking opportunities. Platforms will provide virtual spaces for learners to connect with peers, experts, and mentors from around the world, facilitating knowledge sharing and the exchange of ideas. This global network of learners will create a vibrant community of lifelong learners, contributing to continuous professional development and innovation.

In conclusion, the future of online education and e-learning platforms holds immense potential. The integration of advanced technologies, personalized learning experiences, and global networking opportunities will redefine the educational landscape. As individuals embrace online education, they will have the flexibility to learn at their own pace, acquire practical skills, and connect with a global community of learners. The future of education is online, and it promises to unlock new possibilities for individuals to thrive in the ever-evolving job market.

Lifelong Learning and Continuous Skill Development

In the post-pandemic job market, lifelong learning and continuous skill development have become essential for individuals to stay competitive and adapt to the evolving industry demands. As job roles transform and new technologies emerge, the ability to embrace a mindset of continuous learning is crucial for enhancing employability and career growth.

Platforms like LinkedIn Learning exemplify the resources available for lifelong learning. These platforms offer a wide range of courses on diverse topics, including technical skills, leadership, and personal development. Professionals can access these learning resources to stay updated and acquire relevant knowledge and skills that are in demand in the job market.

The transformation in education, particularly the rise of remote learning, has revolutionized the accessibility and flexibility of education. Online learning platforms provide individuals with opportunities to acquire new skills and knowledge from the comfort of their own homes, at their own pace. This accessibility eliminates geographical barriers and allows individuals to engage in continuous learning, irrespective of their location.

As the job market evolves, individuals must embrace continuous learning to remain competitive. New technologies, industry trends, and changing job requirements demand that individuals regularly update their skills and adapt to emerging opportunities. By cultivating a commitment to lifelong learning, individuals can proactively respond to these changes and position themselves for career success.

Continuous skill development not only enhances individual

employability but also contributes to personal growth and fulfilment. It enables individuals to stay relevant in their fields, take on new challenges, and explore new avenues. Lifelong learners are more adaptable, resilient, and capable of navigating the uncertainties of the job market.

In conclusion, lifelong learning and continuous skill development have become imperative in the post-pandemic job market. Online learning platforms provide accessible and flexible resources for individuals to acquire new skills and stay ahead of industry trends. By embracing a mindset of lifelong learning, individuals can enhance their employability, adapt to evolving demands, and ensure long-term career success in an ever-changing world.

CHAPTER XVII.
REMOTE LEARNING
AND EDUCATION

Transformations in Education and Remote Learning

In the post-pandemic job market, education has undergone significant transformations, primarily driven by the shift towards remote learning. Educational institutions and professionals have swiftly adapted to remote teaching and learning methodologies, leveraging digital tools and platforms to facilitate online education. This transformation has not only ensured continuity of education during challenging times but has also opened new opportunities for individuals to acquire knowledge and skills from the comfort of their own homes.

A real-world example of the impact of remote learning can be seen in the surge of enrolment on platforms like Coursera during the pandemic. As people sought to upskill and reskill, Coursera experienced a significant increase in the number of individuals accessing their platform. Coursera offers a wide range of courses from top universities and institutions, providing learners with flexible options to acquire knowledge and skills in various domains.

The shift to remote learning has brought several benefits. Firstly, it has improved accessibility by eliminating geographical constraints, allowing individuals from different locations to access quality education. Moreover, remote learning has provided flexibility, enabling learners to pace their education according to their schedules. This has been particularly beneficial for working professionals and those with other commitments.

Digital tools and platforms have played a crucial role in facilitating remote learning. Video conferencing tools, learning management systems, and online collaboration platforms have enabled interactive and engaging virtual classrooms. Educational materials, including lectures, assignments, and assessments, have been digitized, making them easily accessible and adaptable to different learning styles.

While remote learning has its advantages, it also presents challenges. Lack of reliable internet access and technological infrastructure can hinder the participation of individuals from underserved communities. Additionally, the absence of in-person interactions and face-to-face engagement can affect the social and emotional aspects of learning.

In conclusion, the post-pandemic job market has witnessed a significant transformation in education, with the rapid adoption of remote learning. Platforms like Coursera have provided individuals with access to a diverse range of courses and flexible learning options. The integration of digital tools and platforms has enhanced accessibility and flexibility in education. As remote learning continues to evolve, it is essential to address challenges and ensure inclusivity to maximize the benefits of this transformation in the world of education.

The Future of Online Education and E-Learning Platforms

The future of education is increasingly being shaped by the integration of online learning and e-learning platforms. These platforms offer accessible and flexible learning opportunities, allowing individuals to learn at their own pace and from anywhere in the world. With advancements in technology, online education is becoming more immersive and interactive, incorporating elements such as virtual reality (VR) and augmented reality (AR) to enhance the learning experience.

A real-world example of the future of online education can be seen in the success of Udacity, an e-learning platform that offers nano-degree programs in collaboration with industry leaders. These programs focus on practical skills and provide learners with the opportunity to work on real-world projects, preparing them for the demands of the job market.

The integration of VR and AR technologies holds tremendous potential for online education. These technologies can create realistic and engaging virtual environments, allowing learners to interact with content in a more immersive way. For example, medical students can simulate surgical procedures using VR, and engineering students can visualize complex structures using AR. This not only enhances understanding but also provides hands-on experience that is crucial for practical learning.

E-learning platforms are also leveraging data analytics and machine learning algorithms to personalize the learning experience. By analysing learner data, platforms can provide customized recommendations, adaptive assessments, and targeted feedback, catering to the individual needs and learning styles of learners. This personalized approach promotes deeper engagement and improves learning outcomes.

Furthermore, online education is breaking down barriers to access education, particularly for individuals in remote or underserved areas. The flexibility of online learning allows individuals to overcome geographical limitations and learn from renowned institutions and instructors from around the world. This democratization of education ensures that quality learning opportunities are available to a wider audience.

However, the future of online education also brings challenges. Ensuring the quality and credibility of online courses, addressing the digital divide, and fostering social interactions and networking opportunities in a virtual environment are some of the areas that require attention.

In conclusion, the future of education lies in the integration of online learning and e-learning platforms. With advancements in technology, online education is becoming more immersive, personalized, and accessible. Platforms like Udacity are leading the way by offering practical-focused programs that align with industry demands. As we move forward, it is important to harness the potential of emerging technologies and address challenges to unlock the full potential of online education in the future.

Lifelong Learning and Continuous Skill Development

In the post-pandemic job market, lifelong learning and continuous skill development have become essential for individuals to stay competitive and adapt to changing industry demands. As job roles evolve and new technologies emerge, individuals need to embrace a mindset of continuous learning to enhance their employability.

A real-world example of a platform that promotes lifelong learning is LinkedIn Learning. This platform offers a wide range of courses on various topics, including technical skills, leadership, and personal development. Professionals can access relevant and up-to-date learning resources to stay ahead in their careers.

The transformations in education, particularly the rise of online learning, have revolutionized the accessibility and flexibility of education. Remote learning allows individuals to acquire new skills and knowledge from the comfort of their own homes.

Online learning platforms provide a wealth of resources and opportunities for individuals to upskill and reskill, preparing them for the demands of the post-pandemic job market.

Lifelong learning is no longer optional but a necessity in today's rapidly changing world. As technologies advance and industries evolve, individuals must continuously update their skills to remain relevant. This includes acquiring new technical skills, staying updated on industry trends, and developing essential soft skills such as adaptability, critical thinking, and communication.

Continuous skill development not only enhances employability but also opens new career opportunities. Employers value individuals who demonstrate a commitment to learning and self-improvement. By continuously expanding their knowledge and skills, individuals can position themselves as valuable assets to their organizations and increase their chances of career advancement.

Moreover, lifelong learning goes beyond formal education. It encompasses informal learning through self-study, online courses, workshops, conferences, and networking opportunities. Individuals should actively seek opportunities to learn and grow, both within and outside their current roles.

In conclusion, lifelong learning and continuous skill development are crucial for individuals to thrive in the post-pandemic job market. Online learning platforms like LinkedIn Learning provide accessible and up-to-date resources for individuals to upskill and adapt to changing industry demands. By embracing a mindset of continuous learning, individuals can enhance their employability, seize new career opportunities, and navigate the evolving world of work with confidence.

XVI. The Role of Government and Policies in Shaping the Future of Work

Government Initiatives to Support Job Creation and Economic Recovery

Government initiatives play a crucial role in supporting job creation and facilitating economic recovery in the post-pandemic job market. These initiatives aim to stimulate economic growth, provide financial assistance to businesses, and create an environment conducive to job creation. Governments may implement various strategies, such as tax incentives, grants, and subsidies, to encourage businesses to expand their operations and hire new employees.

A real-world example of a government initiative is the Paycheck Protection Program (PPP) launched by the United States government during the COVID-19 pandemic. This program provided forgivable loans to small businesses, enabling them to retain and rehire employees. This initiative aimed to support job retention and prevent widespread unemployment during the economic downturn.

Government initiatives to support job creation and economic recovery are not limited to financial assistance programs. Governments also play a crucial role in creating policies and regulations that promote a favourable business environment. This includes reducing bureaucratic hurdles, streamlining processes, and implementing pro-business policies that encourage investment and entrepreneurship.

Furthermore, governments can invest in infrastructure development projects to stimulate job creation. Initiatives such as building new transportation systems, investing in renewable energy infrastructure, and improving digital connectivity can create employment opportunities and drive economic growth.

Government initiatives also extend to promoting workforce development and upskilling programs. By investing in education and training initiatives, governments can equip individuals with the skills needed to succeed in the evolving job market. This includes providing access to vocational training, supporting apprenticeship programs, and collaborating with educational institutions and industry partners to align skills with industry demands.

In conclusion, government initiatives are crucial in supporting job creation and facilitating economic recovery in the post-pandemic job market. By providing financial assistance, creating a favourable business environment, investing in infrastructure, and promoting workforce development, governments can play a significant role in stimulating economic growth and reducing unemployment. These initiatives not only provide immediate relief but also contribute to long-term economic resilience and a thriving job market.

Policies for Reskilling and Upskilling the Workforce

In response to the evolving job market, governments worldwide are recognizing the importance of reskilling and upskilling the workforce. Policies are being developed to ensure that individuals have access to the necessary resources, training programs, and educational opportunities to acquire new skills or enhance existing ones. These policies focus on promoting lifelong learning, bridging the skills gap, and equipping individuals with the capabilities needed for emerging industries and technologies.

A real-world example of a government initiative in this domain is the SkillsFuture program in Singapore. This program aims to empower individuals to develop skills throughout their lives. It provides funding support for training courses, encourages collaboration between educational institutions and industry partners, and promotes the recognition of skills and competencies. The SkillsFuture program encourages individuals to embrace continuous learning and acquire new skills to stay relevant in the evolving job market.

Policies for reskilling and upskilling the workforce also involve partnerships between governments, educational institutions, and businesses. Governments collaborate with educational institutions to develop curriculum that aligns with industry needs, ensuring that individuals gain skills that are in demand. They also work with businesses to identify skill gaps and develop training programs that address those gaps.

Furthermore, policies for reskilling and upskilling often include initiatives to provide financial assistance to individuals, especially those from disadvantaged backgrounds to access training programs. This ensures that everyone has an equal opportunity to acquire the skills necessary for employment in emerging industries.

In conclusion, policies for reskilling and upskilling the workforce are crucial in preparing individuals for the changing job market. By promoting lifelong learning, bridging the skills gap, and providing resources and support for training programs, governments can empower individuals to acquire new skills or enhance existing ones. These policies not only benefit individuals by increasing their employability but also contribute to economic growth and competitiveness.

Balancing Technological Advancements with Social Welfare

As technological advancements continue to shape the future of work, governments face the challenge of ensuring that social welfare remains a priority. Policies are required to address the ethical implications of automation, protect workers' rights, and mitigate the potential negative impacts on employment and income inequality. Governments play a crucial role in establishing regulations, promoting fair labour practices, and safeguarding workers' well-being in the face of rapid technological change.

A real-world example of a policy framework that addresses the balance between technological advancements and social welfare is the General Data Protection Regulation (GDPR) in Europe. This policy protects individuals' data privacy and governs how organizations handle personal information. By establishing clear rules and regulations regarding data protection, the GDPR ensures that individuals' rights are respected, and their data is handled responsibly. This policy not only enhances individuals' privacy but also fosters trust in the digital economy and safeguards against potential data breaches.

The chapter highlights the pivotal role of government and policies in shaping the future of work. Through initiatives that support job creation and economic recovery, governments provide the necessary foundation for a thriving job market. Policies for reskilling and upskilling the workforce enable individuals to adapt to changing demands and acquire the skills required for emerging industries.

Additionally, governments must strike a balance between technological advancements and social welfare to ensure fair practices and protect workers' rights. This involves establishing regulations to address issues such as job displacement, worker safety, and income inequality caused by automation. Governments can also promote social safety nets and provide support for workers affected by technological disruptions.

In conclusion, as technology continues to advance, governments have a responsibility to ensure that social welfare remains a priority. By implementing policies that protect workers' rights, address ethical implications, and promote fair labour practices, governments can strike a balance between technological advancements and social welfare. Understanding the role of government and the impact of policies empowers individuals to navigate the post-pandemic job market with resilience and adaptability.

CHAPTER XIX.
WORKPLACE HEALTH AND SAFETY IN THE POST-PANDEMIC ERA

Adapting Workspaces for Health and Safety

The post-pandemic era calls for a renewed focus on workplace health and safety. Employers must implement measures to create a safe and healthy working environment for employees. This includes adhering to physical distancing guidelines, providing personal protective equipment (PPE), and implementing enhanced cleaning and sanitization protocols. Workspaces may be reconfigured to allow for better ventilation, fewer touchpoints, and the promotion of hygiene practices.

A real-world example of a company that has effectively adapted its workspace for health and safety is Google. They have implemented social distancing measures by reconfiguring office layouts, staggering work shifts, and implementing strict cleaning protocols. These measures ensure the well-being of their employees and reduce the risk of COVID-19 transmission in the workplace.

In addition to physical changes, employers are also encouraged to provide education and training on health and safety practices. This includes educating employees on proper hand hygiene, respiratory etiquette, and the importance of staying home when feeling unwell. Clear communication channels should be established to keep employees informed about any updates or changes related to health and safety protocols.

The adaptation of workspaces for health and safety not only protects employees' physical well-being but also contributes to their overall sense of security and confidence in the workplace. It helps to mitigate the spread of infectious diseases, promotes employee well-being, and fosters a positive work environment.

Furthermore, the implementation of health and safety measures can have long-term benefits beyond the pandemic. By prioritizing the well-being of employees, employers can improve productivity, reduce absenteeism, and enhance employee retention and loyalty.

In conclusion, adapting workspaces for health and safety is crucial in the post-pandemic era. Employers must implement measures to create a safe and healthy working environment, including physical distancing, PPE provision, and enhanced cleaning protocols. By prioritizing employee well-being, employers can foster a positive work environment and contribute to the long-term success of their organizations.

Mental and Physical Well-being Initiatives in the Workplace

The well-being of employees goes beyond physical safety. Employers should prioritize mental and emotional well-being by providing resources and support programs. This includes access to counselling services, mental health awareness campaigns, and flexible work arrangements to promote work-life balance. Physical well-being initiatives such as wellness programs, ergonomic assessments, and fitness facilities can also contribute to a healthier workforce.

A real-world example of a company that prioritizes mental

and physical well-being is Salesforce. They offer employee assistance programs that provide confidential counselling services for mental health support. These programs ensure that employees have access to the necessary resources and professional guidance to address their mental health concerns. Additionally, Salesforce provides wellness programs, including yoga and mindfulness sessions, to promote employee well-being and reduce stress. These initiatives contribute to a positive work environment and support employees in maintaining their mental and physical well-being.

By investing in mental and physical well-being initiatives, employers can create a supportive and inclusive work environment. This, in turn, leads to increased employee satisfaction, engagement, and productivity. When employees feel supported in their well-being, they are more likely to perform at their best and experience a better work-life balance.

Furthermore, prioritizing well-being in the workplace has long-term benefits for both employees and organizations. It can reduce absenteeism, improve retention rates, and enhance the overall organizational culture. Employees who feel valued and supported in their well-being are more likely to stay with the company, contributing to the stability and success of the organization.

In conclusion, mental and physical well-being initiatives are crucial in the workplace. Employers should provide resources and support programs to promote employee well-being, including mental health support, flexible work arrangements, and wellness programs. By prioritizing well-being, employers create a positive work environment and foster a healthier, more engaged workforce.

Strategies for Crisis Management and Future Preparedness

Workplace health and safety must include strategies for

crisis management and future preparedness. Employers should develop comprehensive contingency plans to address potential emergencies and mitigate risks. This involves establishing communication protocols, conducting regular drills, and ensuring access to essential resources in times of crisis. Being prepared for various scenarios helps organizations navigate unforeseen challenges and ensure business continuity.

A real-world example of organizations implementing crisis management strategies is their response to the COVID-19 pandemic. Many organizations developed business continuity plans that included remote work protocols, communication strategies, and contingency plans for disruptions in supply chains. These measures allowed businesses to adapt quickly and continue operations during the crisis. Companies that had proactive crisis management plans in place were better equipped to respond to the challenges posed by the pandemic.

The chapter emphasizes the importance of workplace health and safety in the post-pandemic era. Adapting workspaces to prioritize health and safety, promoting mental and physical well-being, and implementing strategies for crisis management and future preparedness are essential for creating a resilient and thriving work environment.

By prioritizing employee well-being and preparedness, organizations can foster a culture of trust, productivity, and resilience. This enables employees to feel supported and confident in their ability to navigate challenges. It also contributes to the overall stability and success of the organization.

Moreover, having crisis management strategies in place enhances the organization's ability to respond effectively to emergencies, minimize disruptions, and protect the well-being of employees. Proactive planning and preparation enable organizations to adapt quickly, communicate effectively, and make informed decisions during times of crisis.

In conclusion, workplace health and safety encompass strategies for crisis management and future preparedness. Employers should develop comprehensive contingency plans, establish effective communication protocols, and ensure access to essential resources. By prioritizing preparedness, organizations create a resilient work environment that can effectively navigate unforeseen challenges and ensure business continuity.

CHAPTER XX. AUGMENTED REALITY AND VIRTUAL REALITY IN THE WORKPLACE

Applications of AR and VR in Training and Simulations

Augmented Reality (AR) and Virtual Reality (VR) have emerged as powerful tools for enhancing training and simulations in the workplace. By overlaying digital information in the real world or creating immersive virtual environments, AR and VR provide unique opportunities for experiential learning and skill development. Industries such as manufacturing, healthcare, and aviation have embraced these technologies to train employees in realistic, yet safe, environments. AR and VR can simulate complex procedures, allow for interactive training modules, and offer real-time feedback, leading to more effective learning outcomes.

A real-world example of AR and VR applications in the healthcare sector is surgical training. Medical professionals can use these technologies to practice complex procedures in a virtual environment before performing them on actual patients. This allows for realistic simulations and provides a safe space for medical professionals to gain hands-on experience without risking patient safety. By using AR and VR, medical professionals can refine their skills, learn new techniques, and improve their overall surgical proficiency.

Similarly, AR and VR are being utilized in other industries such as manufacturing, where employees can receive training on operating complex machinery and equipment in a virtual setting. This enables them to gain practical experience and familiarize themselves with intricate processes, reducing the risk of accidents and errors in real-world scenarios. In aviation, pilots can undergo flight simulations using VR to practice emergency procedures, navigation, and landing in various conditions, improving their skills and decision-making abilities.

The use of AR and VR in training and simulations offers numerous benefits. It provides a highly immersive and interactive learning experience, allowing individuals to engage with virtual scenarios and practice tasks in a realistic yet controlled environment. AR and VR can also offer real-time feedback, enabling learners to identify and correct mistakes instantly. Moreover, these technologies can accommodate different learning styles and cater to individual training needs, making learning more personalized and effective.

In conclusion, AR and VR have revolutionized training and simulations in various industries. By providing immersive and interactive experiences, these technologies enhance skill development, improve learning outcomes, and enhance workplace safety. The application of AR and VR in training empowers employees with practical experience and confidence, ultimately leading to increased efficiency and productivity in the workplace.

Enhancing Remote Collaboration and Communication through AR and VR

AR and VR technologies have the potential to enhance remote collaboration and communication in the post-pandemic work environment. With the rise of remote work, AR and VR can bridge the physical distance by creating virtual meeting spaces and enabling realistic interactions among remote team members. Virtual collaboration platforms can replicate the experience of working together in a shared office space, fostering teamwork, creativity, and innovation.

A real-world example of a collaboration platform that utilizes AR and VR is Spatial. This platform enables remote teams to meet in virtual spaces and collaborate on projects as if they were physically present. Participants can share and interact with digital content in real-time, fostering seamless communication and collaboration. By leveraging AR and VR, teams can visualize and manipulate 3D models, annotate documents, and engage in immersive discussions, leading to more effective collaboration and problem-solving.

AR and VR technologies enable remote teams to feel more connected and engaged by creating a sense of presence and shared experience. These technologies can overcome the limitations of traditional video conferencing tools by immersing participants in virtual environments that mimic real-world interactions. Team members can explore virtual spaces, gesture, and communicate non-verbally, enhancing the richness and depth of communication. This fosters a greater sense of connection, trust, and engagement among remote team members.

Additionally, AR and VR can be used for remote training and onboarding processes. New employees can undergo virtual onboarding experiences where they can interact with virtual mentors, explore virtual office environments, and familiarize themselves with company culture and workflows. This immersive approach to onboarding enhances the learning experience and accelerates the integration of new team members into the organization.

In conclusion, AR and VR technologies have the potential to revolutionize remote collaboration and communication. By creating virtual meeting spaces and enabling realistic interactions, these technologies enhance teamwork, creativity, and innovation among remote teams. The use of AR and VR in remote work settings fosters a sense of presence and shared experience, leading to increased engagement and productivity. As remote work continues to be a prevalent trend, integrating AR and VR into collaboration tools can unlock new possibilities for effective remote collaboration and communication.

Future Possibilities of Immersive Technologies in the Workplace

The future of work holds tremendous potential for the widespread adoption of immersive technologies such as Augmented Reality (AR) and Virtual Reality (VR). As these technologies continue to evolve, we can envision a workplace where employees can access information and data through wearable AR devices, visualize and manipulate 3D models in real time, and conduct virtual meetings and conferences in immersive environments. The possibilities are endless and can revolutionize industries such as architecture, design, marketing, and customer service, creating new possibilities for customer engagement, product development, and problem-solving.

A real-world example of the application of AR and VR in the architecture and design industry showcases their transformative potential. Architects and designers can use AR and VR to create immersive experiences for clients, allowing them to virtually walk through buildings, visualize interior designs, and make informed decisions before construction begins. This enhances client engagement, streamlines the design process, and reduces costly iterations.

In the future workplace, wearable AR devices can provide

employees with real-time information, overlaying digital content onto their physical environment. This can enhance productivity and efficiency by providing instant access to relevant data, instructions, and guidance. For example, field service technicians can use AR to access manuals, troubleshooting guides, and real-time data overlays while performing maintenance tasks, improving accuracy, and reducing downtime.

Immersive technologies also hold promise for remote collaboration and communication. Virtual meetings and conferences in VR environments can recreate the feeling of being physically present, enabling realistic interactions and fostering collaboration among geographically dispersed teams. With the use of avatars and spatial audio, participants can engage in virtual discussions, brainstorming sessions, and collaborative problem-solving, promoting creativity and innovation.

Moreover, AR and VR can revolutionize training and professional development. From technical skills to soft skills training, these technologies provide immersive and interactive learning experiences. Employees can practice real-world scenarios, receive instant feedback, and engage in realistic simulations that enhance knowledge retention and skill acquisition.

In conclusion, the future of work is ripe with possibilities for the integration of immersive technologies such as AR and VR. These technologies have the potential to transform industries, improve productivity, and drive innovation. From enhancing customer experiences to revolutionizing remote collaboration and training, the applications of immersive technologies in the workplace are vast and promising. Embracing these technologies can unlock new opportunities for organizations to stay ahead in the ever-evolving world of work.

CHAPTER XXI.
CYBERSECURITY AND DATA PRIVACY IN THE DIGITAL AGE

Importance of Cybersecurity in a Digitized Work Environment

In the post-pandemic job market, where remote work and digital technologies have become the norm, ensuring robust cybersecurity measures is of utmost importance. The increasing reliance on digital platforms and online communication exposes organizations to various cyber threats, such as data breaches, phishing attacks, and ransomware. A strong cybersecurity framework is necessary to protect sensitive information, maintain business continuity, and safeguard against financial and reputational damage.

A real-world example that highlights the critical need for organizations to prioritize cybersecurity is the Colonial Pipeline cyberattack in May 2021. This attack, which targeted one of the largest fuel pipelines in the United States, disrupted the fuel supply across the eastern part of the country. It resulted in significant economic and logistical challenges, demonstrating the severe impact cyber threats can have on critical infrastructure and daily operations. This incident serves as a stark reminder that organizations must remain vigilant and proactive in defending against cyber threats.

Implementing effective cybersecurity measures involves multiple layers of protection. Organizations should invest in robust firewalls, secure network infrastructure, and encryption technologies to safeguard data in transit and at rest. Regular security audits and vulnerability assessments can help identify weaknesses and address them promptly. Employee awareness and training programs are crucial in educating staff about cybersecurity best practices, such as recognizing phishing attempts, using strong passwords, and following secure remote work protocols.

Furthermore, organizations should establish incident response plans to effectively handle cyber incidents and mitigate their impact. These plans should outline the steps to be taken in the event of a security breach, including incident reporting, containment, and recovery procedures. Regular backups of critical data should also be maintained to ensure quick restoration in case of a ransomware attack or data loss.

In conclusion, the importance of cybersecurity in a digitized work environment cannot be overstated. Organizations must recognize the risks associated with increased digitalization and take proactive steps to protect their systems, data, and operations. By implementing robust cybersecurity measures, organizations can minimize the likelihood of successful cyber-attacks, safeguard sensitive information, and ensure the smooth functioning of their business. Prioritizing cybersecurity is not only a necessity but also a strategic advantage in the evolving landscape of work.

Protecting Sensitive Data and Preventing Cyber Threats

In the digital age, protecting sensitive data and preventing cyber threats is paramount for organizations. The increasing sophistication of cybercriminals and the evolving threat landscape necessitate comprehensive cybersecurity strategies. By implementing robust measures, organizations can safeguard sensitive data, maintain the trust of their customers, and mitigate the risk of financial and reputational damage.

A real-world example that underscores the importance of protecting sensitive data is the WannaCry ransomware attack in 2017. This global cyberattack affected hundreds of thousands of computers by exploiting a vulnerability in outdated software. The incident highlighted the need for organizations to regularly update their software and apply security patches to prevent such attacks. It serves as a reminder that maintaining up-to-date systems and implementing security best practices are essential in mitigating cyber threats.

To protect sensitive data, organizations must establish strong network security measures. This includes using firewalls, intrusion detection and prevention systems, and secure web gateways to monitor and control network traffic. Encryption techniques should be employed to protect data both in transit and at rest, ensuring that even if intercepted, the data remains secure and unreadable.

Multi-factor authentication (MFA) adds an extra layer of security by requiring additional verification beyond just a username and password. By implementing MFA, organizations can significantly reduce the risk of unauthorized access to sensitive systems and data. Regular software updates and patch management are crucial in addressing known vulnerabilities and protecting against the exploitation of security flaws.

Employee training and awareness programs play a vital role in preventing cyber threats. Human error is often exploited by cybercriminals through techniques such as phishing emails and social engineering. Educating employees about the latest cyber threats, promoting strong password practices, and encouraging them to report suspicious activities are essential components of a robust cybersecurity strategy.

In conclusion, protecting sensitive data and preventing cyber threats requires a multi-layered approach. Organizations must invest in network security, encryption, multi-factor authentication, and regular software updates. Equally important is the cultivation of a cybersecurity-aware culture through employee training and awareness programs. By implementing comprehensive cybersecurity strategies, organizations can effectively safeguard sensitive data and minimize the risk of cyber threats in the digital landscape.

Compliance with Data Privacy Regulations and Best Practices

In the digital age, compliance with data privacy regulations and best practices is crucial for organizations. With growing concerns about data protection and privacy, individuals are becoming more aware of their rights and are demanding that their personal information be handled responsibly. Organizations must prioritize compliance to build trust with their customers, protect sensitive data, and avoid legal and reputational risks.

One prominent example of data privacy regulation is the European Union's General Data Protection Regulation (GDPR). The GDPR sets strict rules for how organizations handle personal data, including obtaining explicit user consent, providing transparency in data processing, and implementing appropriate security measures. Non-compliance with the GDPR can result in severe financial penalties and reputational damage. This regulation highlights the need for organizations to prioritize data privacy and take proactive steps to ensure compliance.

To comply with data privacy regulations and best practices, organizations should adopt privacy-by-design principles. This involves integrating data protection measures into the design and development of products, services, and systems from the outset. By implementing privacy-by-design, organizations can embed privacy and security controls into their operations, minimizing the risk of data breaches and privacy violations.

Secure data storage and transmission are also essential for data privacy. Organizations should implement encryption technologies to protect data at rest and in transit. Additionally, they should regularly assess and update their security measures to address emerging threats and vulnerabilities. This includes conducting vulnerability assessments, penetration testing, and implementing security patches and updates promptly.

Compliance with data privacy regulations requires ongoing efforts, including staff training and awareness programs. Employees should be educated about data privacy regulations, best practices, and their responsibilities in handling personal data. Organizations should establish clear data privacy policies and procedures, providing employees with guidance on how to handle and protect personal information.

In conclusion, compliance with data privacy regulations and best practices is a critical aspect of maintaining data security and building trust with customers. Organizations must prioritize data privacy by obtaining consent, implementing privacy-by-design principles, and ensuring secure data storage and transmission. By complying with data privacy regulations, organizations can demonstrate their commitment to protecting sensitive data and enhance their reputation in the post-pandemic job market.

CHAPTER XXII.
FUTURE OF WORK: ETHICAL CONSIDERATIONS AND SOCIAL IMPACT

Ethical Challenges in the Future of Work

As we move forward into the future of work, it is essential to address the ethical challenges that arise from technological advancements and changing work dynamics. Automation, artificial intelligence (AI), and robotics have the potential to revolutionize industries, but they also bring forth ethical dilemmas that need careful consideration.

One of the key concerns is job displacement and economic inequality. The adoption of automation and AI technologies may lead to the elimination of certain job roles, potentially resulting in unemployment and income disparities. It is crucial to address these challenges by promoting reskilling and upskilling programs, providing support for affected workers, and ensuring that the benefits of technological advancements are shared more equally.

Ethical considerations also arise in the use of decision-making algorithms. Algorithms can impact various aspects of work, such as hiring decisions, performance evaluations, and resource allocation. It is essential to ensure that these algorithms are designed and implemented in a fair, transparent, and accountable manner, free from biases and discrimination. Regular audits and oversight can help mitigate potential ethical risks associated with algorithmic decision-making.

Privacy and surveillance are additional ethical concerns in the future of work. The increasing use of technologies such as facial recognition and biometric identification raises questions about data privacy, consent, and potential abuses of surveillance power. Regulations and guidelines must be established to safeguard individual privacy rights and prevent the misuse of personal data.

Real-world examples, such as the ethical debate surrounding facial recognition technology, highlight the need for ethical considerations. Concerns regarding privacy, surveillance, and potential biases in identification and profiling have spurred discussions about the responsible use of these technologies.

In conclusion, the future of work brings forth ethical challenges that need to be addressed proactively. By promoting fair and inclusive practices, ensuring transparency and accountability in decision-making algorithms, protecting privacy rights, and fostering equality in the face of automation, we can shape a future of work that is both technologically advanced and ethically sound. By incorporating ethical considerations into the development and implementation of emerging technologies, we can strive for a future where innovation and progress go hand in hand with social responsibility and ethical values.

Balancing Automation and Job Displacement with Social Responsibility

As automation continues to shape the future of work,

it is essential to strike a balance between technological advancements and social responsibility. While automation can increase efficiency, productivity, and profitability for businesses, it also raises concerns about job displacement and its impact on workers and communities. To ensure a fair and inclusive transition, it is crucial to prioritize social responsibility in the face of automation.

One key aspect of balancing automation and job displacement is rethinking education and reskilling programs. As certain job roles become automated, workers may need to acquire new skills to remain employable in the changing job market. Governments, educational institutions, and companies must collaborate to provide accessible and affordable reskilling and upskilling opportunities for affected workers. By investing in lifelong learning programs, individuals can adapt to new roles and industries, minimizing the negative impact of job displacement.

Creating new job opportunities in emerging fields is another critical aspect of social responsibility in the face of automation. While certain jobs may be replaced by machines, new roles will emerge that require human skills such as creativity, critical thinking, and emotional intelligence. Policies and initiatives should be implemented to foster the growth of these emerging industries, creating employment opportunities that align with human capabilities and providing a safety net for workers affected by job displacement.

Companies and policymakers also have a responsibility to consider the social impact of automation decisions. It is important to implement policies that promote inclusive growth and ensure that the benefits of automation are shared equitably. This may involve measures such as offering fair wages, providing job security, and establishing mechanisms for worker participation and representation in decision-making processes.

A real-world example of addressing job displacement due to automation can be seen in Amazon's implementation of robotic systems in its warehouses. This technology resulted in job losses for human workers. In response, Amazon has taken steps to invest in upskilling programs to help employees transition to higher-skilled roles within the company. This demonstrates a commitment to social responsibility by supporting workers through the changing landscape of automation.

In conclusion, balancing automation and job displacement with social responsibility is crucial for creating a future of work that is fair, inclusive, and sustainable. By rethinking education and reskilling programs, creating new job opportunities, and implementing policies that prioritize social well-being, we can navigate the challenges of automation while ensuring that workers and communities thrive in the evolving job market. Through collaboration between governments, businesses, and individuals, we can shape a future where technological advancements benefit society.

Ensuring Equity and Fairness in the Evolving Job Market

As the job market continues to evolve, it is crucial to prioritize equity and fairness to prevent the widening of socioeconomic disparities. Achieving a level playing field for all individuals requires addressing biases, promoting diversity and inclusion, and providing equal opportunities for career growth and advancement. By implementing policies and initiatives that support marginalized groups and underrepresented communities, we can work towards creating a more inclusive and equitable future of work.

One key area that requires attention is the need to address biases in recruitment and hiring processes. Unconscious biases can create barriers for individuals from diverse backgrounds, limiting their access to job opportunities. Organizations should implement strategies such as blind hiring practices, diverse candidate slates, and training programs to mitigate biases and ensure fair consideration for all applicants.

Promoting diversity and inclusion is another essential aspect of ensuring equity in the job market. Companies should strive to create inclusive work environments where individuals from diverse backgrounds feel valued and have equal opportunities to contribute and grow. This includes fostering a culture of respect, providing resources for employee affinity groups, and implementing diversity and inclusion training programs.

Equal opportunities for career growth and advancement are crucial for ensuring fairness in the job market. Organizations should provide mentorship programs, professional development opportunities, and transparent promotion processes to empower all employees to reach their full potential. By addressing barriers and biases that impede career progression, organizations can foster an environment where merit and skills are rewarded irrespective of an individual's background.

The gender pay gap and underrepresentation of women in leadership positions are persistent challenges that require attention. Organizations must adopt gender equity measures, conduct regular pay equity audits, and implement policies that promote equal opportunities for career progression. By dismantling systemic barriers and fostering a supportive environment, we can create a more equitable job market for everyone.

In conclusion, ensuring equity and fairness in the evolving job market is essential for creating a more inclusive and just society. By addressing biases, promoting diversity and inclusion, and providing equal opportunities for career growth, we can create a job market where everyone has a fair chance to succeed. Through collective efforts from organizations, policymakers, and individuals, we can shape a future of work that embraces diversity, promotes equity, and drives positive social change.

CHAPTER XXIII.
WORK-LIFE INTEGRATION AND FLEXIBILITY

Redefining Work-Life Balance in the Post-Pandemic Era

The COVID-19 pandemic has brought significant changes to the way we work and has challenged traditional notions of work-life balance. In the post-pandemic era, it is crucial to redefine work-life balance as work-life integration. This new approach recognizes that work and personal life are interconnected and aims to create harmony between the two, rather than striving for a strict separation.

Work-life integration emphasizes flexibility, autonomy, and the ability to prioritize personal well-being alongside professional responsibilities. With remote work becoming more prevalent, individuals can structure their work schedules to accommodate personal commitments and achieve a better balance. This might involve flexible work hours, allowing individuals to work when they are most productive or when it suits their personal needs.

Organizations play a key role in redefining work-life balance by adopting policies and practices that support work-life integration. Companies like Google and Microsoft have recognized the importance of this shift and have implemented initiatives to promote flexibility and well-being. They offer flexible work arrangements, unlimited vacation time, and family-friendly benefits to support employees in achieving healthy work-life integration.

In addition to flexible work arrangements, promoting employee well-being is essential in the post-pandemic era. This includes providing resources and support for mental health, promoting work-life boundaries, and encouraging regular breaks and time off. Employers can also foster a culture that values work-life integration by setting clear expectations, promoting open communication, and recognizing the importance of personal well-being in driving overall productivity and job satisfaction.

It is important to note that work-life integration does not mean constantly being available or working excessively. It is about finding a sustainable balance that allows individuals to meet their personal and professional commitments while maintaining their well-being.

In conclusion, redefining work-life balance as work-life integration is essential in the post-pandemic era. This approach recognizes the interconnected nature of work and personal life and emphasizes flexibility, autonomy, and well-being. By adopting supportive policies and fostering a culture that values work-life integration, organizations can create an environment where individuals can thrive both personally and professionally.

Flexible Work Arrangements and Remote Work Policies

The COVID-19 pandemic has revolutionized the way we work, leading to the widespread adoption of flexible work arrangements and remote work policies. Companies across industries have realized the benefits of remote work and are implementing policies that provide employees with the flexibility to choose where and when they work. This shift has transformed traditional work structures and has significant implications for the future of work.

Remote work offers numerous advantages for both employees and employers. For employees, it provides the flexibility to work from the comfort of their own homes or any location of their choice, eliminating long commutes and enhancing work-life balance. It also opens opportunities for individuals who may face geographical limitations or have personal commitments that require flexibility. For employers, remote work can increase employee satisfaction, improve retention rates, and access a global talent pool. It can also lead to cost savings in terms of office space and infrastructure.

One company that has embraced remote work is Automattic, the organization behind WordPress. Automattic operates on a fully distributed model, with employees working remotely from different locations worldwide. This model has allowed them to tap into a diverse talent pool and build a global workforce while promoting flexibility and work-life balance.

However, remote work also presents challenges that organizations must address. It requires effective communication and collaboration tools to ensure seamless connectivity and teamwork. Companies must establish clear expectations, set guidelines for remote work, and provide the necessary support and resources for employees to thrive in a remote work environment.

As we navigate the post-pandemic job market, it is evident that flexible work arrangements and remote work policies will continue to play a crucial role. Organizations that embrace these approaches will not only attract top talent but also create an inclusive work environment that values work-life balance and employee well-being.

In conclusion, the pandemic has accelerated the adoption of flexible work arrangements and remote work policies. Companies like Automattic have demonstrated the benefits of a fully distributed model, fostering flexibility and access to a global talent pool. As the future of work evolves, organizations must continue to prioritize remote work infrastructure, effective communication, and work-life balance to create a thriving and productive workforce.

Strategies for Work-Life Integration and Employee Well-being

In the post-pandemic job market, maintaining work-life integration and promoting employee well-being has become paramount for organizations. To achieve this, companies can implement various strategies that foster a healthy balance between work and personal life while prioritizing the well-being of their employees.

One effective strategy is to cultivate a culture that values work-life balance. This involves promoting a supportive work environment where employees feel encouraged to set boundaries and manage their time effectively. Employers can lead by example by modelling healthy work-life integration and recognizing the importance of personal well-being. This culture shift can be reinforced through regular communication, emphasizing the value of personal time, and discouraging overwork or burnout.

Establishing clear boundaries between work and personal life is crucial for maintaining work-life integration. Encouraging employees to define specific work hours and non-work hours helps create separation and ensures that personal time is respected. Employers can discourage after-hours communication and encourage employees to disconnect from work-related tasks during their designated non-work periods.

To support employee well-being, organizations can provide resources and initiatives that address mental and physical health. This can include wellness programs, access to mental health resources, and opportunities for physical activity. Companies like LinkedIn offer wellness programs, mental health resources, and flexible work arrangements to support work-life integration and employee well-being.

Additionally, offering flexible scheduling options can greatly contribute to work-life integration. Flexibility allows employees to adapt their work schedules to accommodate personal obligations or preferences, promoting a sense of control and balance. This can be achieved through remote work options, flexible hours, or compressed workweeks.

Professional development opportunities should also be provided to support employee growth and fulfilment. By offering avenues for learning, skill development, and career advancement, organizations demonstrate their commitment to employee well-being and foster a sense of purpose and satisfaction in the workplace.

In conclusion, organizations must prioritize work-life integration and employee well-being in the post-pandemic job market. By fostering a culture of work-life balance, establishing clear boundaries, providing resources for mental and physical health, offering flexible scheduling options, and supporting professional development, companies can create an environment that promotes employee well-being and maximizes productivity. Recognizing the importance of work-life integration and implementing strategies to support it will lead to a happier, more engaged workforce and contribute to the overall success of the organization.

CHAPTER XXIV.
ARTIFICIAL
INTELLIGENCE AND
WORK AUTOMATION

Impacts of AI on Job Roles and Tasks

The advent of Artificial Intelligence (AI) is reshaping job roles and tasks across various industries, revolutionizing the way we work. While AI brings numerous benefits, it also raises concerns about job displacement and the evolving nature of work. This chapter examines the impacts of AI on different job roles and tasks, exploring both the opportunities and challenges it presents.

In the healthcare industry, AI is transforming medical imaging and diagnosis. AI-powered medical imaging systems can analyse vast amounts of medical images, assisting radiologists in detecting abnormalities and diagnosing diseases more accurately and efficiently. This improves patient outcomes by reducing diagnostic errors and enhancing the speed of diagnosis. However, radiologists may need to shift their focus towards complex cases that require human expertise, as AI handles routine scans.

In manufacturing, AI-powered robots and automation systems have the potential to streamline production processes and increase efficiency. These robots can perform repetitive and physically demanding tasks with precision and speed, freeing up human workers to focus on more complex and creative aspects of production. While some manual labour jobs may be replaced by AI, new roles will emerge, such as AI system operators and maintenance technicians.

AI also impacts the financial sector, where algorithms and machine learning algorithms are used for fraud detection, risk assessment, and algorithmic trading. AI-driven chatbots and virtual assistants have transformed customer service, provided personalized assistance, and resolved queries efficiently. However, the role of human financial analysts and advisors remains crucial in interpreting AI-generated insights, making strategic decisions, and building relationships with clients.

While AI automates routine tasks, it also opens opportunities for upskilling and reskilling. Individuals can acquire new skills that complement AI technologies, such as data analysis, AI programming, and human-machine interaction. By embracing lifelong learning and adapting to the changing job landscape, individuals can leverage AI to enhance their capabilities and remain relevant in the workforce.

In conclusion, AI is reshaping job roles and tasks across industries, offering opportunities for increased efficiency, accuracy, and productivity. While concerns about job displacement exist, the evolving nature of work calls for a proactive approach to upskilling and reskilling. By embracing the potential of AI and acquiring new skills, individuals can thrive in a workforce that embraces the power of human-AI collaboration. Organizations and policymakers must also ensure a smooth transition by providing support and training programs to facilitate the integration of AI into the workforce.

Human-AI Collaboration in the Workplace

The integration of Artificial Intelligence (AI) into the workplace is not about replacing humans but rather fostering collaboration between humans and machines. Human-AI collaboration harnesses the unique strengths of both to achieve better outcomes, improve productivity, and unlock new opportunities for innovation. This chapter explores the potential benefits and challenges of human-AI collaboration in the workplace.

Virtual assistants like Siri and Alexa exemplify human-AI collaboration. These voice-activated AI systems assist users by providing information, managing tasks, and performing simple requests. By working alongside humans, virtual assistants streamline daily tasks, making them more convenient and efficient. They exemplify how AI can augment human capabilities and enhance productivity.

In data analysis and decision-making, AI can assist humans by processing vast amounts of data quickly and accurately. AI algorithms can identify patterns, trends, and insights that humans may miss, enabling data-driven decision-making. For example, in financial services, AI algorithms can analyse market trends and make investment recommendations, which humans can evaluate and act upon. This collaboration between humans and AI enhances decision-making capabilities and improves overall performance.

In creative fields, AI can inspire and augment human creativity. AI-powered tools can generate ideas, assist in design tasks, or provide suggestions for content creation. For instance, AI algorithms can assist writers by generating text based on specific inputs or providing design recommendations for graphic designers. This collaboration allows humans to leverage AI's computational power and generate innovative and high-quality work.

However, human-AI collaboration also presents challenges. Ethical considerations, such as bias in AI algorithms or the impact on employment, need to be addressed. Ensuring transparency, accountability, and fairness in AI systems is crucial for effective collaboration. Additionally, organizations must provide appropriate training and support to help employees adapt to working with AI technologies.

In conclusion, human-AI collaboration in the workplace offers significant benefits in terms of productivity, decision-making, and innovation. By leveraging AI's computational capabilities and augmenting human skills, organizations can achieve better outcomes. However, addressing ethical concerns and providing adequate support to employees is essential for successful collaboration. The future of work lies in harnessing the potential of human-AI collaboration to create a more efficient, innovative, and inclusive work environment.

Ethical Considerations in AI Adoption and Automation

As the adoption of Artificial Intelligence (AI) in the workplace increases, it is crucial to address the ethical considerations that arise. Issues such as privacy, bias, transparency, and accountability must be carefully considered to ensure responsible AI adoption. This chapter explores the ethical implications of AI in work automation and emphasizes the need for ethical guidelines and regulations to govern its use.

Real-world examples, such as Amazon's facial recognition software, highlight the potential biases in AI algorithms. If not properly addressed, these biases can result in unfair profiling and discrimination. It is essential to develop AI systems that are transparent, accountable, and unbiased, ensuring fairness and equal treatment for all individuals.

Privacy is another key ethical concern in AI adoption. As AI relies on data, ensuring the protection of individuals' privacy becomes paramount. Organizations must implement robust data protection measures, obtain informed consent, and handle data responsibly and ethically.

Transparency is critical in AI systems. Users should have a clear understanding of how AI algorithms work, how decisions are made, and the limitations of the technology. Transparent AI systems build trust and allow individuals to assess the fairness and reliability of AI-driven decisions.

Accountability is also crucial when it comes to AI adoption. Organizations must be accountable for the actions and consequences of AI systems. They should have mechanisms in place to rectify any errors, address biases, and provide avenues for recourse when AI systems fail or produce unintended outcomes.

To navigate these ethical considerations, the development of guidelines and regulations is necessary. Ethical frameworks can guide organizations in the responsible and ethical use of AI. Regulatory bodies and industry standards can ensure compliance with ethical principles and hold organizations accountable for their AI practices.

In conclusion, as AI adoption and automation continue to shape the future of work, it is essential to address the ethical implications that arise. Privacy, bias, transparency, and accountability must be considered and upheld to ensure responsible AI adoption. By developing ethical guidelines, regulations, and industry standards, organizations can harness the potential of AI while safeguarding individuals' rights, promoting fairness, and maintaining trust in the technology.

CHAPTER XXV. THE GIG ECONOMY: CHALLENGES AND OPPORTUNITIES

Gig Work Trends and Their Implications

The emergence of the gig economy has revolutionized the job market, presenting a range of trends and implications for workers. This chapter examines the trends in gig work, including the growing number of independent contractors, freelancers, and platform-based gig workers. It also explores the implications of these trends on job security, income stability, and benefits.

Real-world examples, such as ride-sharing platforms like Uber and Lyft, illustrate the transformative impact of the gig economy. These platforms have provided flexible income opportunities for drivers, allowing them to work on their terms. However, they have also raised concerns about worker rights and fair compensation. The classification of gig workers as independent contractors rather than employees has led to debates surrounding benefits, job security, and access to social protections.

One implication of gig work is the potential erosion of job security. Gig workers often lack the stability and protections associated with traditional employment. The absence of long-term contracts and the reliance on short-term gigs can create financial uncertainty and vulnerability. Additionally, gig workers may face challenges in accessing benefits such as healthcare, retirement plans, and unemployment insurance.

Income stability is another consideration in gig work. While gig work offers flexibility, the fluctuating nature of gig earnings can make it challenging to maintain a steady income. Gig workers may experience periods of high demand and income, but they can also face periods of low demand and financial instability.

The rise of gig work also has broader implications for the labour market. Traditional job structures and employment relationships are being redefined, and industries are adapting to new workforce dynamics. This presents both opportunities and challenges for workers, businesses, and policymakers to ensure fair and sustainable working conditions.

In conclusion, the trends in gig work have reshaped the job market, offering new possibilities for flexibility and income generation. However, they also pose challenges related to job security, income stability, and benefits. As the gig economy continues to evolve, it is crucial to address these implications and find ways to strike a balance between flexibility and worker protection.

Balancing Flexibility and Job Security in the Gig Economy

The gig economy has disrupted traditional employment models by providing individuals with flexible work opportunities. This chapter delves into the challenges faced by gig workers in balancing flexibility and job security, as well as explores strategies to mitigate these challenges.

Platforms like Upwork and Fiverr have revolutionized the gig economy, allowing individuals to offer their skills and services to a global client base. The flexibility to choose projects and work on their terms is a major draw for gig workers. However, this flexibility often comes at the expense of job security and access to traditional employment benefits.

To strike a balance between flexibility and job security, gig workers can adopt various strategies. Building a diversified client base is crucial to mitigate the risks associated with relying on a single source of income. By cultivating multiple clients and projects, gig workers can reduce the impact of fluctuations in demand and ensure a more stable income stream.

Investing in professional development is another key strategy for gig workers. By continuously upgrading their skills and expanding their expertise, gig workers can enhance their marketability and remain competitive in a rapidly changing job market. This proactive approach to self-improvement can lead to increased job opportunities and long-term success in the gig economy.

Furthermore, gig workers can consider forming professional networks and communities to foster collaboration, share resources, and gain insights from peers. These networks provide a sense of community and support, allowing gig workers to navigate the challenges of the gig economy more effectively.

In conclusion, balancing flexibility and job security is a crucial consideration for gig workers. While the gig economy offers freedom and autonomy, it is essential to implement strategies that mitigate the risks associated with job instability. By diversifying client bases, investing in professional development, and fostering professional networks, gig workers can navigate the gig economy with greater confidence and achieve a better balance between flexibility and job security.

Legal and Policy Considerations for Gig Workers

The gig economy has brought about significant changes to the traditional employment landscape, creating the need for legal and policy considerations specific to gig workers. This chapter explores the complex legal and policy issues surrounding gig work, focusing on the ongoing debate regarding worker classification and the need for updated labour laws.

One of the primary challenges in the gig economy is determining the proper classification of gig workers - whether they should be considered employees or independent contractors. This classification has implications for worker rights, benefits, and legal protections. While some argue that gig workers should be classified as employees to ensure access to benefits and protections, others emphasize the importance of maintaining the flexibility and autonomy that gig work provides.

A notable example is the passing of Assembly Bill 5 (AB5) in California, which aimed to reclassify gig workers as employees. This decision sparked a national conversation about the gig economy and worker rights, with proponents advocating for fair treatment and protections for gig workers.

In addition to worker classification, there is a growing recognition of the need for updated labour laws and regulations that address the unique circumstances and rights of gig workers. This includes considerations such as minimum wage, working hours, occupational safety, and access to benefits like healthcare and retirement plans. Policymakers are exploring new approaches to strike a balance between protecting gig workers and supporting the flexibility that is inherent in gig work.

By addressing legal and policy considerations for gig workers, society can ensure fair treatment, protect workers' rights, and promote a more inclusive and equitable gig economy. Policymakers need to engage in ongoing discussions and collaborations with stakeholders to develop comprehensive regulations that meet the evolving needs of the gig workforce.

In conclusion, the legal and policy considerations surrounding gig work are vital for ensuring fair treatment and protection for gig workers. The ongoing debate over worker classification and the need for updated labour laws reflect the complexities and importance of addressing the unique challenges posed by the gig economy. By navigating these considerations, policymakers can promote a gig economy that balances flexibility and worker rights, ultimately fostering a more sustainable and inclusive job market for gig workers.

CHAPTER XXVI. REMOTE WORK: BEYOND THE PANDEMIC

Long-Term Implications of Remote Work

The COVID-19 pandemic has sparked a significant shift in the way we work, with remote work becoming the new norm for many individuals and organizations. This chapter explores the long-term implications of remote work beyond the pandemic, examining how it has reshaped the traditional office environment and the effects it has on employees and employers.

One of the notable long-term implications of remote work is the transformation of the physical office space. As companies embrace remote work, they are revaluating their real estate needs, downsizing office spaces, and adopting flexible work arrangements. This shift towards remote work has the potential to reduce commuting time, lower carbon emissions, and enable a more sustainable approach to work.

Remote work also offers various benefits for both employees and employers. For employees, it provides increased flexibility, better work-life balance, and the opportunity to work from anywhere. Remote work can also enhance productivity and job satisfaction, as employees have greater autonomy over their work environment and can customize their schedules to suit their preferences.

Employers can benefit from remote work by accessing a broader talent pool, reducing overhead costs, and potentially increasing employee retention rates. Remote work allows companies to tap into talent from different geographical locations, enabling diverse perspectives and skills. Additionally, organizations can save on expenses related to office space, utilities, and other infrastructure.

However, remote work also poses challenges that need to be addressed. Issues such as maintaining team cohesion, fostering collaboration, and managing work-life boundaries require deliberate efforts from both employees and employers. Additionally, remote work may exacerbate feelings of isolation and loneliness, impacting employee well-being and mental health.

Real-world examples from companies like Twitter and Square, which have announced permanent work-from-home policies, demonstrate a shift towards a more remote-friendly work culture. These organizations recognize the long-term potential of remote work and its ability to create a more flexible and inclusive work environment.

In conclusion, remote work has long-term implications that extend beyond the pandemic. It has transformed the traditional office space, providing benefits such as flexibility and increased productivity. However, it also presents challenges that require proactive measures to address. By embracing remote work and adopting strategies to support its effective implementation, organizations can unlock the benefits of this new way of working and create a future that combines the best of remote and in-person collaboration.

Hybrid Work Models and Their Benefits

As organizations adapt to the changing dynamics of the post-pandemic job market, many are considering hybrid work models that combine remote and in-person work. This section explores the benefits of hybrid work and discusses the importance of designing effective policies to cater to the needs of employees while maintaining team collaboration and productivity.

Hybrid work offers increased flexibility, allowing employees to have a mix of remote and in-person work. This flexibility provides individuals with the autonomy to structure their workdays in a way that suits their personal preferences and obligations. It promotes a better work-life balance by reducing commuting time and enabling employees to spend more time with their families or pursue personal interests.

Furthermore, hybrid work models can enhance employee well-being and job satisfaction. Remote work offers a conducive environment for focused work, minimizing distractions and interruptions that can occur in a traditional office setting. On the other hand, in-person work provides opportunities for social interaction, collaboration, and relationship building. By combining these elements, employees can benefit from the advantages of both remote and in-person work.

Organizations can also reap numerous benefits from implementing hybrid work models. Reduced office space requirements can lead to cost savings, as companies may need less physical workspace for employees who work remotely part of the time. Additionally, access to a larger talent pool becomes possible, as geographical limitations are mitigated when remote work is incorporated into the work model.

Real-world examples from companies like Microsoft, which introduced the concept of "hybrid-remote" work, demonstrate the implementation of hybrid work policies. This approach allows employees to work from home for less than 50% of their working week while spending the remaining time in the office for collaboration and in-person meetings. By striking a balance between remote and in-person work, organizations can harness the benefits of both while ensuring effective collaboration and maintaining team cohesion.

In conclusion, hybrid work models offer numerous benefits for employees and organizations alike. By combining remote and in-person work, individuals can enjoy increased flexibility and improved work-life balance, while companies can achieve cost savings and access a broader talent pool. Designing effective hybrid work policies that consider the needs of employees and foster collaboration is essential for organizations to embrace this new way of working successfully.

Strategies for Effective Remote Team Management

Managing remote teams requires new approaches and strategies to ensure effective collaboration, communication, and productivity. This chapter provides practical insights and tips for effective remote team management, covering topics such as fostering communication and collaboration in virtual settings, leveraging digital tools for project management, and promoting employee engagement and well-being in a remote work environment.

One key aspect of remote team management is fostering clear and frequent communication. Regular check-ins, team meetings, and one-on-one sessions can help keep everyone aligned and informed. Leveraging digital communication tools such as video conferencing platforms and instant messaging applications can facilitate real-time communication and promote a sense of connection among team members.

Collaboration is essential for remote teams to work together effectively. Utilizing digital collaboration tools, project management platforms, and shared document repositories enables seamless collaboration and ensures that everyone is working towards shared goals. Encouraging team members to actively contribute their ideas and perspectives promotes a sense of ownership and involvement in the team's success.

Remote work can sometimes lead to feelings of isolation or disengagement. As a manager, it is important to prioritize employee engagement and well-being. Regularly checking in with team members, providing opportunities for virtual team-building activities, and promoting a healthy work-life balance can help create a positive remote work culture.

Real-world examples from companies like Buffer and Zapier, which have implemented remote-first strategies and developed comprehensive remote work playbooks, demonstrate successful remote team management. These companies have prioritized clear communication, established remote work policies, and cultivated a strong company culture that supports remote collaboration.

By exploring the long-term implications of remote work, discussing the benefits of hybrid work models, and providing strategies for effective remote team management, this chapter equips readers with the knowledge and insights to navigate the evolving landscape of remote work in the post-pandemic job market. It offers real-world examples and practical advice to help individuals and organizations thrive in a remote work environment, fostering productivity, engagement, and a sense of connection among remote teams.

CHAPTER XXVII.
UPSKILLING FOR THE
FUTURE OF WORK

Identifying In-Demand Skills for the Future

In the rapidly changing job market, it is essential to identify the skills that will be in high demand in the future. This chapter delves into the evolving skill requirements across various industries and emphasizes the importance of adaptability and agility in acquiring new skills. It discusses the rise of digital skills, such as data analysis, artificial intelligence, and programming, while also highlighting the need for a strong foundation in soft skills, including critical thinking, communication, and problem-solving.

The World Economic Forum's Future of Jobs Report is a valuable resource that provides insights into the skills that will be in demand in the future workplace. It identifies skills such as complex problem-solving, critical thinking, creativity, and emotional intelligence as essential for success. These skills are valuable across industries and are considered foundational for adapting to the evolving demands of the job market.

Digital skills have become increasingly crucial in today's technology-driven world. Skills such as data analysis, artificial intelligence, machine learning, and programming are in high demand across various sectors. As businesses leverage data and automation technologies to drive innovation and efficiency, individuals with a strong digital skill set will have a competitive advantage.

However, it is important to recognize that soft skills remain highly relevant and sought after. Skills like effective communication, collaboration, adaptability, and resilience are essential for navigating a complex and dynamic work environment. These skills enable individuals to effectively interact with others, navigate change, and solve problems creatively.

The chapter emphasizes the importance of continuous learning and skills development to stay relevant in the future job market. Lifelong learning, both in technical and soft skill domains, is crucial for professionals to adapt to emerging technologies, changing industry trends, and evolving job roles. Seeking out opportunities for upskilling and reskilling, such as online courses, workshops, and certifications, is essential to meet the demands of the future workplace.

By understanding the in-demand skills identified by reputable sources like the World Economic Forum and recognizing the value of both digital and soft skills, individuals can proactively prepare themselves for the future job market. Embracing a mindset of continuous learning and adaptability will help individuals thrive in an ever-changing professional landscape, seize new opportunities, and contribute to their personal and professional growth.

Lifelong Learning and Continuous Skill Development

In today's rapidly evolving world, lifelong learning and continuous skill development have become more crucial than ever. This section explores the concept of lifelong learning and the importance of continuously acquiring new skills throughout one's career. It emphasizes the mindset, habits, and strategies necessary to adapt to changing demands and stay ahead of the curve.

Lifelong learning is a mindset that recognizes the need for ongoing skill development and knowledge acquisition throughout one's life. It is about embracing a growth mindset and being open to new ideas, experiences, and learning opportunities. By adopting a mindset of continuous learning, individuals can stay relevant, adapt to new technologies and industry trends, and enhance their professional growth and employability.

Continuous skill development involves actively seeking out opportunities to acquire new skills and expand existing ones. This can be done through various means, such as online courses, professional development programs, workshops, conferences, and mentorship opportunities. These resources provide individuals with the knowledge and tools to upskill and stay competitive in their respective fields.

Online learning platforms like Coursera, LinkedIn Learning, and Udemy have revolutionized access to educational resources by offering a wide range of courses and certifications in diverse disciplines. These platforms enable individuals to learn at their own pace, choose topics that align with their interests and career goals, and acquire new skills conveniently from anywhere in the world.

To engage in lifelong learning effectively, individuals need to cultivate habits such as curiosity, self-motivation, and discipline. They should proactively seek out learning opportunities, set learning goals, and allocate time for continuous skill development. Regular reflection and self-assessment can help identify areas for improvement and guide the selection of relevant learning resources.

Employers also play a crucial role in fostering a culture of lifelong learning within organizations. They can provide employees with access to training programs, mentorship, and development opportunities to support their continuous skill development. By investing in the growth and development of their workforce, organizations can drive innovation, enhance employee engagement, and stay competitive in the dynamic job market.

In conclusion, lifelong learning and continuous skill development are essential for individuals to adapt, grow, and succeed in today's rapidly changing world. By embracing a mindset of lifelong learning, actively seeking out learning opportunities, and leveraging resources such as online courses and professional development programs, individuals can stay ahead of the curve and enhance their professional prospects. The era of lifelong learning offers boundless possibilities for personal and professional growth, enabling individuals to thrive in the ever-evolving job market.

Upskilling Initiatives and Resources for Individuals and Organizations

In the rapidly changing job market, upskilling has become essential for individuals and organizations to stay competitive and adapt to evolving demands. This section explores various initiatives and resources available to support upskilling efforts, both at the individual and organizational levels.

Governments around the world are recognizing the importance of upskilling and have implemented initiatives to support individuals in acquiring new skills. These initiatives may include funding programs, tax incentives, and partnerships with educational institutions to provide accessible and affordable upskilling opportunities. For example, Amazon's Upskilling 2025 initiative is a $700 million commitment to train 100,000 employees for in-demand jobs within the company and in other industries.

Industry partnerships and collaborations also play a crucial role in promoting upskilling. Organizations can partner with educational institutions, industry associations, and training providers to develop tailored upskilling programs that align with the specific needs of their workforce and industry. These partnerships facilitate the development of relevant and up-to-date training resources, ensuring that individuals are equipped with the skills required for the future of work.

At the organizational level, creating a culture of continuous learning and development is key. Employers can invest in employee training programs, provide opportunities for upskilling and reskilling, and support professional development initiatives. This may include mentoring programs, job rotations, and on-the-job training. By prioritizing employee growth and development, organizations foster a skilled and adaptable workforce, enhancing their competitiveness in the market.

Individuals can take advantage of a wide range of resources to upskill and acquire new skills. Online learning platforms, such as Coursera, LinkedIn Learning, and Udemy, offer a vast array of courses and certifications across various disciplines. These platforms enable individuals to learn at their own pace, access relevant and high-quality content, and acquire new skills conveniently from anywhere in the world.

Professional associations and industry networks also provide opportunities for individuals to engage in upskilling. They offer workshops, webinars, and conferences where individuals can learn from industry experts, network with peers, and stay updated on the latest trends and advancements in their field.

In conclusion, upskilling initiatives and resources are crucial for individuals and organizations to thrive in the post-pandemic job market. Governments, industry partnerships, and organizational strategies all contribute to creating a supportive ecosystem for continuous learning and development. By harnessing these resources and taking proactive steps to upskill, individuals can enhance their employability, adapt to changing industry demands, and unlock new career opportunities. Similarly, organizations that prioritize upskilling cultivate a skilled and resilient workforce, driving innovation and ensuring long-term success in the evolving job market.

CHAPTER XXVIII. MENTAL HEALTH AND WELL-BEING IN THE WORKPLACE

Addressing Mental Health Challenges at Work

Maintaining good mental health is vital for overall well-being, and it is equally important in the workplace. This chapter delves into the significance of addressing mental health challenges at work and explores various strategies to create a supportive environment for employees. It discusses the impact of work-related stress, burnout, and anxiety on employee well-being and performance, emphasizing the need for organizations to prioritize mental health.

Work-related stress can have detrimental effects on employees' mental health, leading to decreased productivity and engagement. Burnout, characterized by chronic exhaustion, cynicism, and reduced effectiveness, is a significant concern in today's fast-paced work environments. Anxiety and other mental health disorders also contribute to employee well-being challenges.

To address these issues, organizations are recognizing the importance of prioritizing mental health in the workplace. Creating a supportive environment is crucial, starting with open communication and reducing the stigma around mental health discussions. Encouraging employees to openly discuss their challenges and concerns can foster a culture of understanding and empathy.

Providing access to mental health resources and support is essential. Employee assistance programs (EAPs) offer confidential counselling services and resources to help employees manage stress, improve well-being, and cope with personal and work-related challenges. Companies like Google have implemented programs such as "Search Inside Yourself" to promote emotional intelligence and mindfulness, fostering a positive work environment and supporting employee well-being.

Leadership plays a critical role in addressing mental health challenges. Managers should be trained to recognize signs of mental health issues, provide support, and create a work environment that promotes work-life balance, flexible schedules, and realistic workloads. Encouraging breaks, promoting self-care practices, and offering mental health days can also contribute to employee well-being.

In conclusion, addressing mental health challenges at work is vital for the overall well-being and productivity of employees. By creating a supportive environment, reducing stigma, providing access to resources, and promoting work-life balance, organizations can prioritize mental health and foster a positive work culture. This, in turn, contributes to improved employee satisfaction, engagement, and overall organizational success.

Creating a Supportive and Inclusive Work Culture

Developing a supportive and inclusive work culture is crucial for employee well-being and organizational success. This chapter explores strategies for fostering a culture that promotes inclusivity and support. It emphasizes the importance of diversity, equity, and inclusion in creating a psychologically safe workplace and discusses initiatives that organizations can implement.

Promoting diversity, equity, and inclusion is key to creating an inclusive work culture. Embracing different perspectives, backgrounds, and experiences fosters innovation, creativity, and collaboration. Organizations can implement initiatives such as employee resource groups (ERGs) that provide a platform for underrepresented employees to connect, share experiences, and support each other. ERGs promote a sense of belonging and inclusion, contributing to a supportive work environment.

Mentorship programs can also play a crucial role in fostering an inclusive culture. Pairing employees with mentors who have different backgrounds and experiences can provide guidance, support, and opportunities for growth. Mentors can offer advice, share knowledge, and help mentees navigate challenges, ultimately fostering a sense of support and inclusivity.

Diversity training programs are instrumental in creating awareness and understanding of biases, stereotypes, and microaggressions. They promote empathy, cultural sensitivity, and inclusive behaviours, enhancing the overall work environment. By equipping employees with the knowledge and skills to recognize and challenge unconscious biases, organizations can cultivate a more inclusive and supportive culture.

Real-world examples, such as Salesforce's "Ohana" culture, demonstrate the successful implementation of supportive and inclusive practices. Their emphasis on inclusivity, trust, and support among employees is reflected in the implementation of ERGs and their commitment to providing equal opportunities for all.

In conclusion, creating a supportive and inclusive work culture is essential for the well-being and success of employees and organizations. By embracing diversity, implementing initiatives such as ERGs and mentorship programs, and conducting diversity training, organizations can foster an environment of inclusivity and support. This promotes employee engagement, retention, and productivity, ultimately contributing to a positive and thriving work culture.

Promoting Work-Life Balance and Stress Management

Maintaining a healthy work-life balance is crucial for preserving mental well-being and overall quality of life. This section explores strategies for promoting work-life balance and stress management, emphasizing the importance of setting boundaries, managing workloads effectively, and encouraging self-care practices.

Setting boundaries is essential for achieving work-life balance. Establishing clear guidelines around work hours, breaks, and personal time helps individuals separate work responsibilities from personal life. It involves communicating expectations with colleagues, turning off work-related notifications outside of working hours, and prioritizing personal commitments.

Managing workloads effectively is another key aspect of promoting work-life balance. It involves setting realistic goals, prioritizing tasks, and delegating when necessary. Employers can support their employees by providing adequate resources and support, ensuring that workloads are manageable and not overwhelming.

Encouraging self-care practices is vital for stress management. Organizations can promote well-being by offering wellness programs, organizing mindfulness sessions, and providing resources for mental health support. Encouraging employees to take regular breaks, practice mindfulness or meditation, and engage in activities that promote relaxation and stress reduction can contribute to a healthier work environment.

Flexible work arrangements, such as flexible schedules and remote work options, play a significant role in promoting work-life balance. They provide individuals with the flexibility to manage their work and personal responsibilities more effectively. Companies like Buffer, a fully remote organization, prioritize work-life balance by implementing practices such as unlimited paid time off, regular breaks, and wellness allowances for employees.

By addressing mental health challenges, fostering a supportive and inclusive work culture, and promoting work-life balance and stress management, this chapter aims to raise awareness about the importance of mental well-being in the workplace. It provides practical strategies, real-world examples, and resources to help individuals and organizations prioritize mental health and create a healthier, more productive work environment. By prioritizing work-life balance and stress management, individuals can experience greater job satisfaction, improved mental well-being, and increased productivity.

CHAPTER XXIX. DIVERSITY AND INCLUSION IN THE FUTURE OF WORK

Benefits of Diverse and Inclusive Workplaces

Creating diverse and inclusive workplaces is not only a moral imperative but also a strategic advantage for organizations. This section explores the benefits that diverse and inclusive workplaces bring to organizations and individuals. It emphasizes the positive impact on innovation, creativity, employee engagement, and overall organizational performance.

Research consistently demonstrates that diverse teams outperform homogenous ones. By bringing together individuals from different backgrounds, experiences, and perspectives, diverse teams generate a wider range of ideas and approaches to problem-solving. This diversity of thought leads to increased innovation, creativity, and adaptability, which are critical in today's rapidly changing business landscape.

Inclusive work environments foster a sense of belonging and psychological safety, where individuals feel valued, respected, and empowered to contribute their unique perspectives. This inclusivity improves employee engagement, collaboration, and retention. When employees feel included and supported, they are more likely to be motivated, productive, and committed to their work.

Organizations that prioritize diversity and inclusion also gain a competitive edge in attracting and retaining top talent. A diverse workforce signals an inclusive culture that values diversity and provides equal opportunities for all employees. This attracts individuals who seek an environment where their differences are celebrated, and their contributions are recognized.

Real-world examples demonstrate the benefits of diversity and inclusion initiatives. Microsoft's Autism Hiring Program is one such example. By embracing neurodiversity and creating an inclusive environment for individuals on the autism spectrum, Microsoft has tapped into their unique skills and perspectives. This initiative has resulted in increased innovation, productivity, and the development of more inclusive products and services.

In conclusion, diverse and inclusive workplaces bring numerous benefits to organizations and individuals. They foster innovation, creativity, and problem-solving capabilities, improve employee engagement and retention, and enhance overall organizational performance. By embracing diversity and creating an inclusive culture, organizations can position themselves for success in the future of work.

Strategies for Building Diverse Teams and Fostering Inclusion

Creating diverse teams and fostering inclusion is essential for organizations to unlock the full potential of their workforce. This section explores strategies and best practices for building diverse teams and fostering inclusion within the workplace. It emphasizes the importance of inclusive recruitment, leadership, and development programs.

To build diverse teams, organizations should adopt inclusive recruitment practices. This involves widening the candidate pool by actively seeking candidates from underrepresented groups and leveraging diverse sourcing channels. It also requires combating unconscious biases by implementing structured interview processes, anonymizing resumes, and providing unconscious bias training to hiring managers. Additionally, forming diverse interview panels can ensure a fair and objective evaluation of candidates.

Inclusive leadership plays a crucial role in fostering an inclusive work culture. Leaders should prioritize diversity and inclusion as core values and lead by example. This includes promoting open communication, actively listening to diverse perspectives, and empowering employees to bring their authentic selves to work. Mentoring and sponsorship programs can also be implemented to provide support and opportunities for career advancement for underrepresented individuals.

Organizations can further foster inclusion by establishing employee resource groups (ERGs) or affinity groups. These groups provide a platform for employees to connect, share experiences, and advocate for diversity and inclusion. ERGs can also play a role in organizing events, training programs, and initiatives that promote understanding and appreciation of different cultures and identities.

IBM serves as an example of a company that has successfully implemented a comprehensive diversity and inclusion strategy. Their approach includes targeted recruiting efforts to attract diverse talent, the establishment of employee resource groups, and leadership development programs. By prioritizing diversity and inclusion, IBM has created a more diverse workforce that fosters innovation, creativity, and collaboration.

In conclusion, building diverse teams and fostering inclusion requires a deliberate and strategic approach. Organizations should implement inclusive recruitment practices, prioritize inclusive leadership, and provide opportunities for mentoring and sponsorship. By embracing diversity and fostering an inclusive work culture, organizations can create an environment where all employees feel valued, empowered, and able to contribute their best.

Overcoming Biases and Promoting Equality in the Workplace

Promoting equality in the workplace requires addressing biases that can hinder fairness and inclusivity. This section explores the impact of unconscious biases on decision-making processes and provides strategies for overcoming biases and creating a more equitable work environment.

Unconscious biases are implicit associations or stereotypes that affect our judgments and decision-making without our conscious awareness. These biases can influence hiring decisions, performance evaluations, and opportunities for career advancement. To overcome biases, organizations can implement awareness training programs to educate employees about the existence and impact of unconscious biases. This training raises awareness and helps individuals recognize and challenge their biases, promoting fair and unbiased decision-making.

In addition to awareness training, organizations should implement inclusive policies and practices that promote equality. This includes ensuring diverse representation on selection panels, establishing clear criteria for evaluation, and providing opportunities for diverse voices to be heard and valued. Creating a culture that embraces diversity and inclusion fosters an environment where different perspectives are appreciated and considered in decision-making processes.

Allyship and advocacy are also essential in promoting equality. Allies actively support and amplify the voices of underrepresented individuals, challenging biases and advocating for equal opportunities. This can be done by speaking up against discriminatory practices, actively seeking diverse perspectives, and supporting initiatives that promote diversity and inclusion.

Adobe serves as an example of an organization that has taken steps to overcome biases. They have implemented unconscious bias training for their employees to raise awareness and challenge biases in decision-making processes. This initiative has contributed to creating a more inclusive and equitable work environment at Adobe.

By highlighting the benefits of diversity and inclusion, providing strategies for building diverse teams, and discussing ways to overcome biases, this chapter empowers individuals and organizations to create a workplace that values equality and harnesses the power of diversity. By actively challenging biases and fostering inclusivity, organizations can build a more equitable work environment where every individual has equal opportunities to thrive and contribute their best.

CHAPTER XXX. REMOTE LEADERSHIP AND TEAM COLLABORATION

Leading and Managing Remote Teams Effectively

Leading and managing remote teams requires a unique set of skills and strategies to ensure team cohesion, productivity, and engagement. This chapter focuses on the best practices for leading remote teams in the post-pandemic job market, addressing the challenges and opportunities that arise in virtual work environments.

Setting clear expectations is crucial when leading remote teams. Communicate goals, deliverables, and performance expectations to ensure everyone is on the same page. Establishing regular communication channels is equally important to maintain team collaboration and connectivity. Utilize video conferences, instant messaging platforms, and project management tools to facilitate seamless communication and foster a sense of connection among team members.

Providing support and guidance is essential in remote team management. Regular check-ins and one-on-one meetings can help team leaders understand individual needs, provide feedback, and help when needed. Leaders should be available to answer questions, provide direction, and offer support, ensuring that remote team members feel supported and valued.

Effective delegation is key to distributing workload and optimizing productivity in remote teams. Assign tasks based on individual strengths and capabilities, while considering workload distribution and deadlines. Provide clear instructions, expectations, and timelines to ensure everyone understands their responsibilities and can work independently.

Fostering a sense of community and belonging within remote teams is critical for engagement and morale. Encourage virtual team-building activities, such as virtual coffee breaks or team bonding sessions, to create opportunities for social interaction and relationship-building. Celebrate achievements and recognize team members' contributions to maintain a positive team culture.

HubSpot serves as an example of an organization that has implemented effective remote team management practices. Their Remote Work Playbook emphasizes proactive communication, frequent check-ins, and fostering a culture of trust and autonomy. By following these guidelines, HubSpot has successfully managed its remote teams and maintained high levels of productivity and employee satisfaction.

By addressing the skills and strategies needed for effective remote team leadership, this chapter equips leaders with the knowledge and tools to navigate the challenges and harness the opportunities of managing remote teams in the post-pandemic job market. By adopting best practices and leveraging technology, leaders can foster collaboration, engagement, and success in their remote teams.

Building Trust and Communication in Virtual Environments

Building trust and effective communication are essential

components of successful remote team collaboration. This section explores strategies for cultivating trust in virtual environments and fostering open and transparent communication among team members.

Regular and transparent communication is a foundational element of trust-building in remote teams. Establishing clear channels for communication, such as video conferences, chat platforms, and project management tools, promotes accessibility and encourages collaboration. Providing regular updates, sharing information, and being responsive to team members' inquiries create a culture of transparency and inclusivity.

Active listening is crucial in virtual environments to ensure that team members feel heard and valued. Encourage active participation during team meetings and discussions and provide opportunities for everyone to share their ideas and perspectives. Demonstrating genuine interest in others' opinions and being receptive to feedback cultivates a sense of trust and respect within the team.

Open and honest discussions are essential for effective communication in virtual environments. Encourage team members to express their thoughts, concerns, and challenges openly, creating a safe space for dialogue. Emphasize the importance of constructive feedback and address conflicts proactively to foster a positive team dynamic.

Empathy and understanding play a vital role in building trust and rapport in virtual teams. Acknowledge and validate team members' experiences and challenges, recognizing that everyone's circumstances may differ. Encouraging empathy fosters a supportive work culture where team members feel valued and understood.

Buffer serves as an example of a company that practices effective communication in a virtual environment. Their use of asynchronous communication tools, such as Slack and Twist, allows their globally distributed team to stay connected and engaged. By prioritizing accessible communication platforms, Buffer ensures that all team members have access to information and can contribute to team discussions, building trust and promoting collaboration.

By implementing strategies for building trust, encouraging open and honest communication, and fostering empathy in virtual environments, teams can cultivate a strong sense of trust and camaraderie, leading to enhanced collaboration and productivity.

Tools and Techniques for Remote Team Collaboration

This section of the chapter explores the tools and techniques that can enhance remote team collaboration and facilitate effective communication and productivity in virtual environments.

Project management software plays a crucial role in remote team collaboration. Platforms like Asana, Trello, and Monday.com allow teams to organize tasks, assign responsibilities, track progress, and collaborate on projects in a centralized and accessible manner. These tools promote transparency, accountability, and efficient workflow management.

Video conferencing platforms are essential for virtual meetings and real-time collaboration. Tools like Zoom, Microsoft Teams, and Google Meet enable face-to-face communication, screen sharing, and interactive discussions. Video conferencing platforms create a sense of connection and allow teams to maintain regular communication and engagement.

Virtual whiteboards and visual collaboration tools are valuable for remote teams engaged in brainstorming sessions and ideation. Platforms like MURAL, Miro, and Lucidspark provide digital canvases where team members can visually map ideas, share feedback, and collaborate on projects. These tools foster creativity, encourage active participation, and enable teams to work together in a virtual workspace.

Best practices for conducting virtual meetings include setting clear agendas, establishing guidelines for participation, and leveraging video and chat features to engage attendees. Utilizing breakout rooms for small group discussions, using collaborative note-taking tools like Google Docs, and recording meetings for reference and accessibility are also effective techniques.

Team-building activities in remote settings can promote rapport and strengthen relationships among team members. Virtual icebreakers, online games, and collaborative challenges foster a sense of camaraderie and create opportunities for social interaction and engagement.

MURAL serves as an example of a digital collaboration platform that enhances remote team collaboration. With its virtual whiteboard and visual workspace, teams can collaborate and ideate together, facilitating creativity, innovation, and effective remote collaboration.

By leveraging project management software, video conferencing platforms, virtual whiteboards, and employing best practices for virtual meetings and team-building activities, remote teams can overcome geographical barriers and work seamlessly together. These tools and techniques enhance communication, foster collaboration, and enable remote teams to achieve their goals effectively in the post-pandemic job market.

CHAPTER XXXI.
FUTURE OF WORK
IN DIFFERENT
INDUSTRIES

Impacts of Technology and Automation in Various Sectors

This chapter delves into the effects of technology and automation on different industries in the post-pandemic job market, examining the transformative impact of emerging technologies such as artificial intelligence (AI), robotics, and data analytics. It explores both the potential challenges and benefits that arise from technology adoption in sectors like manufacturing, healthcare, retail, finance, and transportation.

In the healthcare industry, technological advancements are revolutionizing the way healthcare services are delivered. Telemedicine platforms and remote monitoring devices allow patients to access medical consultations and monitoring remotely, reducing the need for in-person visits, and improving healthcare access. AI-powered diagnostics and data analytics enable more accurate and efficient diagnoses, leading to improved patient outcomes.

In the manufacturing sector, automation and robotics are streamlining production processes, increasing efficiency, and reducing labour-intensive tasks. While this may lead to job displacement, it also creates new job opportunities in fields such as robotics maintenance and programming. The use of AI and machine learning algorithms in quality control and predictive maintenance enhances product quality and reduces downtime.

The retail industry has experienced significant changes with the rise of e-commerce and digital platforms. AI-powered algorithms and data analytics enable personalized customer recommendations and targeted marketing strategies. Automation technologies like cashier-less checkout systems and inventory management systems improve operational efficiency and enhance the overall customer experience.

In finance, technology has revolutionized processes such as online banking, mobile payments, and algorithmic trading. AI-powered chatbots and virtual assistants provide customer support and enhance self-service options. The use of data analytics and machine learning algorithms improves fraud detection and risk management.

Transportation has also been impacted by technology advancements, with the emergence of autonomous vehicles, smart logistics, and ride-sharing platforms. These innovations improve efficiency, reduce costs, and enhance safety in the transportation sector.

While technology adoption in various sectors brings significant benefits, it also presents challenges such as job displacement and the need for upskilling. To navigate these challenges, organizations and individuals must embrace lifelong learning and continuous skill development to remain competitive in the evolving job market.

By exploring the impacts of technology and automation in different sectors, this chapter provides insights into the changing landscape of work and the skills needed to thrive in a technology-driven world. It highlights the potential for improved efficiency, enhanced customer experiences, and new job opportunities, while also addressing the need for upskilling and adaptation to ensure long-term career success.

Opportunities for Innovation and Growth in Different Industries

This section delves into the opportunities for innovation and growth in various industries as they adapt to the evolving landscape of work. It explores how industries can leverage emerging technologies such as blockchain, the Internet of Things (IoT), and renewable energy to drive innovation, streamline processes, and create new business models. It also emphasizes the importance of entrepreneurship and collaboration between industries to foster innovation and capitalize on emerging opportunities.

In the transportation industry, there is a notable shift towards electric and autonomous vehicles. This transition opens new business models and opportunities in areas such as ridesharing, electric vehicle charging infrastructure, and smart mobility solutions. Companies can explore partnerships and collaborations to create integrated transportation systems that provide seamless and sustainable mobility options.

The healthcare sector presents opportunities for innovation through the adoption of digital health technologies, telemedicine, and remote patient monitoring. These advancements improve access to healthcare services, enhance patient care, and enable personalized treatment options. The integration of AI and data analytics in healthcare systems can lead to more accurate diagnoses, efficient healthcare delivery, and improved patient outcomes.

The financial industry is witnessing disruption through fintech innovations, including digital payments, blockchain technology, and robo-advisors. These technologies enhance financial transactions, improve security and transparency, and provide accessible financial services to underserved populations. Collaboration between traditional financial institutions and fintech start-ups can drive further innovation and create new growth opportunities.

The energy sector offers immense potential for innovation and growth through the adoption of renewable energy sources, smart grid technologies, and energy storage solutions. The shift towards clean and sustainable energy not only addresses environmental concerns but also creates job opportunities in renewable energy infrastructure development and maintenance.

Furthermore, the convergence of industries, such as healthcare and technology, presents opportunities for cross-sector collaboration and innovation. For example, the integration of IoT devices in healthcare enables remote monitoring and personalized care, leading to better health outcomes.

By exploring the opportunities for innovation and growth in different industries, this section provides insights into the potential for creating new business models, improving operational efficiency, and addressing societal challenges. It emphasizes the importance of embracing emerging technologies, fostering entrepreneurship, and fostering collaboration between industries to seize opportunities and drive sustainable growth in the post-pandemic job market.

Case Studies and Examples of Industry-Specific Changes

This section of the chapter presents case studies and examples that illustrate the industry-specific changes and adaptations occurring in the post-pandemic job market. It showcases how organizations within different sectors are embracing technology, adopting flexible work models, and implementing innovative practices to thrive in the evolving landscape. These case studies provide insights into successful transformations, lessons learned, and the impact on the workforce within industries such as hospitality, education, entertainment, and professional services.

One notable case study is Airbnb, a disruptor in the hospitality industry. During the pandemic, when traditional travel was limited, Airbnb adapted its business model by offering online experiences and focusing on long-term rentals. This strategic pivot allowed the company to remain relevant and provide alternative travel options to customers. This case study highlights the importance of agility and innovation in responding to changing market conditions.

In the education sector, the pandemic prompted a significant shift towards online learning. Educational institutions worldwide had to quickly adopt digital platforms and remote teaching methods. For example, universities and schools implemented virtual classrooms, online assessments, and interactive learning tools to ensure continuity of education. This case study underscores the necessity of embracing technology and adapting teaching practices to provide quality education in a remote setting.

The entertainment industry also experienced significant changes. With the closure of movie theatres and live events, streaming platforms and online content consumption soared. Production companies and artists turned to virtual performances, live streams, and interactive experiences to engage audiences. This case study demonstrates the industry's resilience and the potential for new forms of entertainment in a digital world.

In professional services, remote work became the norm for many professionals. Law firms, consulting agencies, and accounting firms successfully transitioned to remote work models, leveraging technology for virtual meetings, collaboration, and document sharing. This case study showcases the adaptability of professional services and the effectiveness of remote work in maintaining productivity and client service.

By examining these case studies and examples, this chapter provides real-world illustrations of industry-specific changes and the strategies organizations have implemented to navigate the post-pandemic job market. It highlights the importance of embracing technology, adopting flexible work models, and fostering innovation to remain competitive and resilient. These examples inspire readers to proactively embrace change, explore new opportunities, and leverage emerging trends to thrive in their respective industries.

CHAPTER XXXII.
ENTREPRENEURSHIP
AND INNOVATION
IN THE FUTURE
OF WORK

Embracing an Entrepreneurial Mindset and Opportunities

In this chapter, we explore the role of entrepreneurship in the future of work. We discuss the importance of adopting an entrepreneurial mindset, which involves embracing creativity, taking calculated risks, and being adaptable in a rapidly changing work environment. We delve into the mindset shift required to identify and seize entrepreneurial opportunities, whether it's starting a new venture or innovating within an existing organization. We also highlight the benefits of entrepreneurship, such as autonomy, the potential for financial rewards, and the ability to make a meaningful impact.

The rise of platforms like Airbnb and Uber showcases how individuals have embraced the entrepreneurial mindset to create successful businesses by leveraging technology and meeting evolving consumer needs. These platforms disrupted traditional industries by offering alternative solutions that addressed gaps in the market. This demonstrates the power of entrepreneurial thinking in identifying opportunities and capitalizing on them.

Embracing an entrepreneurial mindset also enables individuals to adapt and thrive in a rapidly changing work environment. With the increasing pace of technological advancements and market disruptions, individuals who possess an entrepreneurial mindset are better equipped to navigate uncertainty, embrace innovation, and seize emerging opportunities. This mindset encourages continuous learning, creative problem-solving, and the ability to pivot in response to market shifts.

Within organizations, fostering an entrepreneurial culture can drive innovation and intrapreneurship. Intrapreneurs are individuals who exhibit entrepreneurial traits and drive change within an organization. By encouraging employees to think like entrepreneurs, organizations can unlock their innovation potential, encourage initiative, and promote intrapreneurial projects that lead to growth and competitive advantage.

Embracing an entrepreneurial mindset is not limited to starting a business; it is a mindset that can be applied to any role or industry. It involves being proactive, seeking out opportunities for growth and improvement, and embracing a continuous learning mindset. Whether it's identifying new ways to improve processes, developing innovative solutions to customer challenges, or seizing opportunities to lead projects, individuals who adopt an entrepreneurial mindset are better positioned to excel in the future of work.

In conclusion, this chapter highlights the importance of embracing an entrepreneurial mindset in the future of work. By fostering creativity, adaptability, and a willingness to take calculated risks, individuals can identify and seize entrepreneurial opportunities. Whether as entrepreneurs starting their ventures or as intrapreneurs driving innovation within organizations, embracing an entrepreneurial mindset offers autonomy, financial potential, and the ability to make a meaningful impact. As the future of work continues to evolve, individuals who adopt this mindset will be well-equipped to navigate change, embrace innovation, and thrive in a dynamic and entrepreneurial work environment.

Fostering Innovation and Creativity in the Workplace

In this section, we explore the importance of fostering innovation and creativity within organizations. We discuss how innovation drives business growth, improves competitiveness, and enhances employee engagement. We explore strategies for creating a culture of innovation, including encouraging experimentation, fostering diverse perspectives, and providing resources for creative problem-solving. We also examine the role of leadership in promoting a supportive environment that encourages risk-taking and rewards innovative thinking.

Google's "20% time" policy allows employees to spend a portion of their work hours on personal projects, leading to innovative products such as Gmail and Google Maps.

Innovation is essential for organizations to stay competitive and adapt to a rapidly changing business landscape. By fostering a culture of innovation, organizations can encourage employees to think creatively, challenge the status quo, and generate new ideas that drive business growth. A culture that values innovation empowers employees to experiment, take risks, and learn from failures, creating an environment that nurtures creativity.

Creating a culture of innovation starts with leadership. Leaders play a crucial role in setting the tone and expectations for innovation within an organization. They should foster a supportive environment that encourages open communication, collaboration, and idea-sharing. By championing innovation and providing resources and support for creative problem-solving, leaders can inspire employees to think outside the box and contribute their unique perspectives.

Organizations can also foster innovation by promoting diversity and inclusion. Diverse teams bring together different perspectives, experiences, and ideas, fuelling creativity and innovation. By fostering an inclusive culture where all voices are heard and valued, organizations can tap into the full potential of their workforce and foster a rich environment for idea generation and innovation.

Encouraging experimentation is another key strategy for fostering innovation. Organizations can provide employees with the freedom and resources to explore new ideas, test hypotheses, and learn from failures. This can be achieved through initiatives such as hackathons, innovation labs, or designated time for employees to work on personal projects. By allowing employees to pursue their passions and explore new avenues, organizations can unlock their innovative potential.

In conclusion, fostering innovation and creativity in the workplace is crucial for organizations to thrive in the future of work. By creating a culture that encourages experimentation, values diverse perspectives, and provides resources for creative problem-solving, organizations can drive innovation, improve competitiveness, and enhance employee engagement. With leadership support and a supportive environment, employees can unleash their innovative potential and contribute to the success of the organization. Organizations that prioritize innovation and creativity will be better positioned to adapt to change, seize opportunities, and thrive in an increasingly dynamic and competitive business environment.

Strategies for Starting and Growing a Successful Business

In this part of the chapter, we provide practical guidance for aspiring entrepreneurs on how to start and grow a successful business. We cover key steps, such as identifying a viable business idea, conducting market research, creating a business plan, securing funding, and navigating legal and regulatory considerations. We discuss the importance of building a strong network, leveraging mentorship, and continuously learning and adapting to market trends. We also explore the potential challenges and provide insights on overcoming obstacles that entrepreneurs may face along their journey.

The success story of Elon Musk, who co-founded PayPal, Tesla, and SpaceX, demonstrates the power of entrepreneurial vision, resilience, and innovation in creating impactful ventures across different industries.

Starting a business requires careful planning and execution. It begins with identifying a viable business idea that solves a problem or meets a market need. Conducting thorough market research helps entrepreneurs understand their target audience, competition, and market trends. Armed with this knowledge, entrepreneurs can refine their idea and create a compelling value proposition.

Creating a comprehensive business plan is crucial for outlining the business's goals, strategies, and financial projections. It serves as a roadmap that guides decision-making and secures funding from potential investors or financial institutions. Entrepreneurs should also consider legal and regulatory requirements and seek professional advice to ensure compliance with laws and regulations.

Securing funding is often a critical step in starting and growing a business. Entrepreneurs can explore various options, including self-funding, loans, venture capital, or crowdfunding platforms, depending on their business model and financial needs. Building a strong network and leveraging mentorship can also provide valuable guidance, support, and access to resources.

Entrepreneurship is not without challenges. Entrepreneurs may face obstacles such as financial constraints, market competition, and operational complexities. It is important to maintain resilience, adaptability, and a willingness to learn from failures. Continuous learning, staying updated on industry trends, and seeking feedback from customers and mentors can help entrepreneurs refine their business strategies and seize growth opportunities.

In conclusion, starting and growing a successful business requires careful planning, a strong foundation, and a willingness to adapt and innovate. By following key steps, leveraging mentorship and networks, and continuously learning and adapting, aspiring entrepreneurs can increase their chances of success. The entrepreneurial journey may have its challenges, but with the right mindset, resources, and strategies, entrepreneurs can navigate the path to success and make a meaningful impact in the future of work.

CHAPTER XXXIII. SUSTAINABLE WORK PRACTICES AND CORPORATE SOCIAL RESPONSIBILITY

Importance of Sustainability in the Workplace

In this chapter, we explore the significance of sustainability in the post-pandemic job market. We discuss how businesses are increasingly recognizing the importance of sustainable practices to address environmental challenges and meet the expectations of consumers and stakeholders. We delve into the concept of sustainability, highlighting its three pillars: environmental, social, and economic. We examine the potential benefits of adopting sustainable work practices, such as cost savings, enhanced brand reputation, and attracting and retaining top talent.

Sustainability is crucial for the long-term well-being of our planet and future generations. Businesses play a significant role in shaping a sustainable future. By integrating sustainable practices into their operations, organizations can reduce their ecological footprint, conserve resources, and mitigate environmental impacts. This includes adopting energy-efficient technologies, minimizing waste, promoting recycling and circular economy principles, and implementing sustainable supply chain management practices.

In addition to environmental considerations, sustainability encompasses social and economic aspects. Organizations that prioritize social sustainability promote fair labour practices, diversity and inclusion, and community engagement. They prioritize employee well-being, provide a safe and healthy work environment, and contribute positively to the communities in which they operate. Socially responsible businesses prioritize ethical sourcing, and fair trade, and support local suppliers and businesses.

Economically, sustainability can lead to cost savings and improved financial performance. Energy-efficient practices reduce utility costs, while waste reduction and recycling initiatives can result in lower disposal expenses. Embracing sustainability also enhances brand reputation and attracts environmentally conscious consumers who are increasingly seeking products and services from socially and environmentally responsible businesses.

Case studies like Patagonia demonstrate the positive impact of sustainability in the workplace. By investing in sustainable materials, implementing recycling programs, and promoting fair labour practices, Patagonia aligns its business with its environmental and social values. This commitment not only enhances their brand reputation but also attracts environmentally conscious customers and fosters a loyal customer base.

In conclusion, sustainability is of paramount importance in the workplace. By adopting sustainable practices, businesses can contribute to a healthier planet, create positive social impact, and achieve long-term economic success. Embracing sustainability not only benefits the environment but also enhances brand reputation, attracts, and retains top talent, and ensures business resilience in the face of changing societal expectations. The integration of sustainability principles into the core business strategies is essential for organizations to thrive in the post-pandemic job market and contribute to a more sustainable and equitable future.

Integrating Sustainable Practices into Business Operations

In this section, we focus on practical strategies for integrating sustainable practices into various aspects of business operations. We discuss energy efficiency, waste reduction, responsible supply chain management, and the adoption of renewable energy sources. We also explore the role of technology in enabling sustainable practices, such as the use of smart systems for energy management and digital platforms for supply chain transparency. We guide setting sustainability goals, measuring performance, and reporting on sustainability initiatives.

Energy efficiency is a key area for businesses to reduce their environmental impact. This involves implementing energy-saving measures such as LED lighting, optimizing HVAC systems, and adopting energy management systems to monitor and control energy usage. By reducing energy consumption, businesses not only lower their carbon footprint but also realize cost savings through reduced utility bills.

Waste reduction and proper waste management are essential components of sustainable business practices. This includes implementing recycling programs, composting, and reducing single-use plastics. By implementing waste reduction initiatives, businesses can minimize their contribution to landfills, conserve resources, and promote a circular economy. Responsible supply chain management is another critical aspect of integrating sustainability into business operations. This involves evaluating suppliers based on their environmental and social practices, ensuring fair labour conditions, and promoting ethical sourcing. By partnering with sustainable suppliers, businesses can create a more responsible and resilient supply chain.

The adoption of renewable energy sources is an effective way for businesses to reduce their carbon emissions and contribute to a cleaner energy future. Installing solar panels, and wind turbines, or purchasing renewable energy credits can help businesses transition to a low-carbon energy system. Additionally, leveraging technology can enable sustainable practices. Smart systems and automation can optimize energy usage, reduce waste, and improve operational efficiency. Digital platforms and blockchain technology can enhance supply chain transparency, traceability, and accountability.

IKEA serves as an exemplary case study in integrating sustainable practices into business operations. By committing to becoming climate positive by 2030, IKEA is investing in renewable energy, improving energy efficiency in their operations, and sourcing sustainable materials for their products. Their sustainability initiatives not only align with their environmental goals but also enhance their brand reputation and attract environmentally conscious customers.

In conclusion, integrating sustainable practices into business operations is crucial for organizations to minimize their environmental impact and contribute to a more sustainable future. By focusing on energy efficiency, waste reduction, responsible supply chain management, and adopting renewable energy sources, businesses can demonstrate their commitment to sustainability. Leveraging technology and setting clear sustainability goals with performance measurement and reporting mechanisms further strengthen their sustainability efforts. Through these initiatives, businesses can not only drive positive environmental change but also enhance their competitiveness, attract customers, and contribute to a more sustainable and resilient global economy.

Social Responsibility and Environmental Stewardship

In this part of the chapter, we delve into the concept of social responsibility and its intersection with environmental stewardship. We discuss the importance of engaging with local communities, promoting diversity and inclusion, and supporting social causes. We examine how companies can align their values and actions to contribute positively to society and minimize their environmental footprint. We explore the concept of corporate social responsibility (CSR) and highlight the benefits of CSR initiatives, including improved employee morale, brand loyalty, and positive community impact.

Engaging with local communities is an integral part of social responsibility. This involves collaborating with community organizations, supporting local initiatives, and contributing to the well-being of the communities in which businesses operate. By actively participating in community development projects, businesses can build strong relationships, enhance their reputation, and foster a sense of belonging among community members.

Promoting diversity and inclusion is another crucial aspect of social responsibility. Creating an inclusive work environment that embraces diversity not only fosters innovation and creativity but also promotes fairness and equality. By implementing diversity and inclusion initiatives, businesses can attract and retain diverse talent, improve decision-making processes, and better understand the needs of their diverse customer base.

Supporting social causes through philanthropic activities and partnerships is a way for businesses to make a positive impact beyond their immediate operations. This can involve donating a portion of profits to charitable organizations, supporting environmental conservation efforts, or addressing social issues such as poverty, education, or healthcare. These initiatives not only benefit society but also contribute to the overall well-being of employees and enhance brand loyalty among customers who align with the company's values.

The North Face serves as a notable example of a company that embraces social responsibility and environmental stewardship. Through programs like the Explore Fund, The North Face supports organizations working to preserve natural spaces and promotes environmental education. By investing in these initiatives, The North Face aligns its actions with its commitment to environmental conservation and educates the public about the importance of protecting natural resources.

In conclusion, social responsibility and environmental stewardship are integral components of sustainable business practices. By engaging with local communities, promoting diversity and inclusion, and supporting social causes, businesses can contribute positively to society while minimizing their environmental footprint. Corporate social responsibility initiatives not only improve employee morale and brand loyalty but also create a more sustainable and equitable future. By incorporating social responsibility into their core values and practices, businesses can make a meaningful impact and inspire others to follow suit.

CHAPTER XXXIV. WORKFORCE DEVELOPMENT AND TALENT MANAGEMENT

Strategies for Attracting and Retaining Top Talent

In this chapter, we explore the critical role of attracting and retaining top talent in the post-pandemic job market. We discuss strategies that organizations can employ to attract and engage high-performing individuals. We delve into the importance of creating a positive employer brand, showcasing company values and culture, and offering competitive compensation and benefits packages. We also discuss the significance of diversity and inclusion in attracting a diverse pool of talent and fostering innovation.

Creating a positive employer brand is crucial in attracting top talent. This involves effectively communicating the company's values, mission, and culture to prospective employees. By showcasing a strong employer brand through social media, employer review sites, and authentic storytelling, organizations can differentiate themselves and attract individuals who align with their values and vision.

Offering competitive compensation and benefits packages is essential for attracting and retaining top talent. Beyond a competitive salary, organizations can provide additional incentives such as health insurance, retirement plans, professional development opportunities, and flexible work arrangements. By understanding the evolving needs and preferences of employees, organizations can tailor their compensation and benefits packages to attract and retain top talent.

Diversity and inclusion are key factors in attracting a diverse pool of talent and fostering innovation. Organizations that prioritize diversity and inclusion create an environment where individuals from different backgrounds and perspectives feel valued and empowered. By implementing inclusive recruitment practices, promoting diverse leadership, and providing equal opportunities for career growth, organizations can attract high-performing individuals who bring unique insights and contribute to the overall success of the company.

Google serves as a renowned example of an organization that successfully attracts and retains top talent. They offer unique perks such as on-site childcare, flexible work arrangements, and opportunities for personal and professional growth. By prioritizing employee well-being and providing a supportive work environment, Google has established itself as an employer of choice for many talented individuals.

In conclusion, attracting and retaining top talent is crucial for organizational success in the post-pandemic job market. By creating a positive employer brand, offering competitive compensation and benefits packages, and fostering diversity and inclusion, organizations can position themselves as attractive destinations for high-performing individuals. Building a strong talent pool enhances innovation, drives business growth, and strengthens the overall competitiveness of the organization in the evolving job market.

Employee Development and Career Advancement Programs

In this section, we focus on the importance of employee development and career advancement programs in nurturing talent and ensuring long-term success. We explore the various methods organizations can employ to support employee growth, such as mentorship programs, training and development initiatives, and performance feedback mechanisms. We discuss the benefits of investing in employee development, including increased employee satisfaction, improved retention rates, and a skilled and adaptable workforce.

Employee development programs play a crucial role in equipping employees with the necessary skills and knowledge to succeed in their roles and advance their careers. By offering mentorship programs, organizations can pair experienced employees with those who seek guidance, creating a supportive environment for professional growth and learning. Through mentorship, employees gain valuable insights, expand their networks, and receive personalized advice to navigate their career paths effectively.

Training and development initiatives are essential for upskilling and reskilling employees in response to evolving industry trends. By providing access to workshops, seminars, and online learning platforms, organizations enable employees to acquire new skills and stay abreast of industry advancements. LinkedIn, for example, offers its employees learning and development opportunities through LinkedIn Learning, an online platform offering a wide range of courses and resources to enhance professional skills.

Performance feedback mechanisms, such as regular performance evaluations and constructive feedback, are essential for employee development. By providing timely and specific feedback, organizations can help employees identify areas for improvement and provide guidance on how to enhance their skills and performance. Performance feedback also serves as a foundation for career development discussions, enabling employees to set goals, track progress, and plan their career paths within the organization.

Investing in employee development programs has numerous benefits for organizations. It increases employee satisfaction and engagement, leading to higher retention rates and reduced turnover. Employees who feel supported in their professional growth are more likely to be motivated and loyal to the organization. Moreover, a skilled and adaptable workforce contributes to increased productivity and innovation, allowing organizations to stay competitive in a rapidly changing business landscape.

In conclusion, employee development and career advancement programs are crucial for nurturing talent and ensuring long-term success. By implementing mentorship programs, training and development initiatives, and performance feedback mechanisms, organizations create an environment that supports employee growth and enables them to reach their full potential. The benefits of investing in employee development are far-reaching, leading to increased employee satisfaction, improved retention rates, and a skilled workforce that drives organizational success in the dynamic job market.

Building a Strong Employer Brand and Culture

In this part of the chapter, we discuss the significance of building a strong employer brand and culture in attracting and retaining talent. We explore how organizations can cultivate a positive work environment that aligns with employee values and fosters engagement and collaboration. We delve into the importance of communication, recognition, and work-life balance in creating a supportive culture. We also discuss the role of leadership in shaping organizational culture and values.

A strong employer brand is essential for attracting top talent and differentiating an organization in the job market. By developing and promoting a compelling employer brand, organizations can showcase their values, mission, and culture, creating an appealing image that resonates with potential employees. This can be achieved through effective communication channels, such as social media platforms and career websites, where organizations can highlight their unique culture, employee testimonials, and growth opportunities.

Creating a positive work culture is vital for employee satisfaction and retention. Organizations should foster an environment that encourages open communication, collaboration, and transparency. Regular feedback and recognition programs can help employees feel valued and appreciated for their contributions. Additionally, promoting work-life balance by offering flexible work arrangements and supportive policies can enhance employee well-being and improve overall job satisfaction.

Leadership plays a crucial role in shaping organizational culture and values. Leaders should exemplify the desired culture through their actions and behaviours. By demonstrating inclusivity, integrity, and accountability, leaders set the tone for the organization and influence employee attitudes and behaviours. Leaders need to create opportunities for employee development, provide mentorship, and empower individuals to contribute their ideas and expertise.

Zappos, an online shoe, and clothing retailer is renowned for its strong company culture. They prioritize employee well-being, encourage open communication, and create a fun and inclusive work environment. By investing in its culture and emphasizing core values, Zappos has attracted and retained top talent, fostering a sense of loyalty and commitment among its employees.

In conclusion, building a strong employer brand and culture is crucial for attracting and retaining talent. By cultivating a positive work environment, promoting effective communication, recognizing employee contributions, and empowering leadership, organizations can create a compelling employer brand that resonates with top talent. A strong culture that aligns with employee values fosters engagement and collaboration, leading to increased job satisfaction and retention. By prioritizing employer branding and culture, organizations can create a workplace that attracts, nurtures, and retains top talent, driving organizational success in the competitive job market.

CHAPTER XXXV.
THE ROLE OF TECHNOLOGY IN WORKFORCE TRANSFORMATION

Technological Advancements Shaping the Future of Work

In this chapter, we explore the profound impact of technological advancements on the future of work. We discuss emerging technologies such as artificial intelligence, machine learning, automation, and the Internet of Things (IoT) and how they are transforming industries and job roles. We delve into the potential benefits and challenges of these technologies, including increased efficiency, improved decision-making, and concerns about job displacement.

Technological advancements are reshaping the way we work and the nature of jobs across various industries. Artificial intelligence and machine learning algorithms are enabling the automation of routine and repetitive tasks, allowing workers to focus on more complex and creative work. Automation and robotics have revolutionized industries like manufacturing, logistics, and agriculture, leading to increased productivity and cost savings.

Amazon's use of robotics and automation in their fulfilment centres is a prime example of how technology has transformed the logistics industry. By employing robots to assist with order picking, sorting, and packaging, Amazon has significantly increased their operational efficiency and delivery speed. This integration of technology has revolutionized the way goods are processed and shipped, enhancing the overall customer experience.

While technological advancements offer numerous benefits, there are also concerns about job displacement and the need for upskilling and reskilling. As automation and AI become more prevalent, certain job roles may become obsolete or require a shift in skills. However, these technologies also create new job opportunities in emerging fields such as data analysis, cybersecurity, and AI development.

To successfully navigate the future of work, individuals and organizations must adapt to these technological changes. This involves embracing a mindset of continuous learning and upskilling to stay relevant in the digital age. It also requires organizations to invest in training programs and provide opportunities for employees to acquire new skills and adapt to technological advancements.

In conclusion, technological advancements are reshaping the future of work, bringing both benefits and challenges. Industries across the board are leveraging emerging technologies to increase efficiency, improve decision-making, and transform job roles. Companies like Amazon are at the forefront of these technological transformations, utilizing automation and robotics to revolutionize their operations. However, it is important to address concerns about job displacement and ensure that individuals can upskill and reskill to thrive in the changing job market. By embracing technological advancements and investing in continuous learning, individuals and organizations can seize the opportunities presented by these technologies and shape a future of work that is both efficient and fulfilling.

Digital Transformation and Its Impact on Job Roles

In this section, we focus on the concept of digital transformation and how it is reshaping job roles and skill requirements. We discuss the need for employees to adapt to digital tools and technologies, as well as the demand for digital literacy and technical skills. We explore the transformation of traditional job functions and the emergence of new roles, such as data analysts, cybersecurity experts, and UX designers.

Digital transformation refers to the integration of digital technologies into various aspects of business operations, resulting in fundamental changes in how organizations operate and deliver value. As technology continues to advance at a rapid pace, employees must adapt and acquire the necessary digital skills to thrive in the digital era.

One of the key impacts of digital transformation is the transformation of traditional job roles. As manual and repetitive tasks become automated, there is a shift towards roles that require expertise in data analysis, cybersecurity, user experience design, and digital marketing. Companies like Shopify have witnessed this transformation first-hand, as the rise of e-commerce platforms has created a demand for professionals skilled in managing online stores, digital marketing, and optimizing the customer experience.

Moreover, digital transformation has also created new opportunities for remote work and flexible work arrangements. With the advancement of digital tools and communication technologies, employees can collaborate and work from anywhere, transcending geographical boundaries. This shift has expanded the talent pool and provided individuals with the flexibility to balance work and personal life.

However, digital transformation also presents challenges, such as the need for upskilling and reskilling. Employees need to continuously update their skills and stay abreast of new technologies to remain competitive in the job market. Organizations must invest in training programs and create a culture of learning to support employees' professional development.

In conclusion, digital transformation is revolutionizing job roles and skill requirements. Employees need to adapt to digital tools and technologies, acquire digital literacy, and develop technical skills to thrive in the digital era. The emergence of new roles and the transformation of traditional job functions provide opportunities for individuals with the right skills. Organizations must support their employees' upskilling efforts and foster a culture of learning to navigate digital transformation successfully. By embracing digital transformation and investing in the development of digital skills, both individuals and organizations can harness the potential of technology and drive innovation in the future of work.

Leveraging Technology for Productivity and Efficiency

In this section, we delve into strategies for leveraging technology to enhance productivity and efficiency in the workplace. We discuss the importance of embracing digital tools and platforms for collaboration, project management, and communication. We explore the benefits of cloud computing, data analytics, and workflow automation in streamlining processes and improving decision-making. We also address the need for organizations to prioritize data security and privacy in an increasingly digital landscape.

Technology has become an integral part of the modern

workplace, offering a wide range of tools and platforms that can significantly enhance productivity and efficiency. One popular example is Slack, a communication and collaboration platform that enables teams to work seamlessly across different locations and time zones, enhancing productivity and collaboration.

Cloud computing is another technology that has transformed the way businesses operate. It allows organizations to store and access data and applications remotely, eliminating the need for physical servers and providing flexibility and scalability. Cloud-based productivity suites like Google Workspace and Microsoft Office 365 provide collaborative tools for document creation, editing, and sharing, enabling teams to work together in real time.

Data analytics is a powerful tool for organizations to gain insights and make data-driven decisions. By leveraging data analytics tools, businesses can analyse large volumes of data to uncover patterns, trends, and customer preferences. This enables more informed decision-making and can lead to improved efficiency and competitive advantage.

Workflow automation is another area where technology plays a significant role in enhancing productivity. Automating repetitive and manual tasks using software and robotics can free up valuable time for employees to focus on more strategic and value-added activities. This not only improves efficiency but also reduces errors and ensures consistency in processes.

While leveraging technology for productivity and efficiency is essential, organizations must also prioritize data security and privacy. With the increasing reliance on digital tools and the collection of sensitive data, organizations must implement robust cybersecurity measures, adhere to data protection regulations, and educate employees on best practices for data security.

In conclusion, leveraging technology for productivity and

efficiency is crucial in today's digital workplace. By embracing digital tools and platforms, organizations can enhance collaboration, streamline processes, and make data-driven decisions. Cloud computing, data analytics, and workflow automation are just a few examples of technologies that can significantly improve efficiency and drive organizational success. However, organizations must also prioritize data security and privacy to mitigate the risks associated with the digital landscape. By effectively harnessing technology, organizations can stay competitive, adapt to changing market dynamics, and thrive in the post-pandemic job market.

CHAPTER XXXVI. RESILIENCE AND ADAPTABILITY IN THE POST-PANDEMIC JOB MARKET

Navigating Uncertainties and Disruptions in the Job Market

In this chapter, we explore the importance of resilience and adaptability in navigating the uncertainties and disruptions of the post-pandemic job market. The COVID-19 pandemic has caused unprecedented disruptions, leading to job losses, remote work, and shifts in consumer behaviour. As a result, individuals need to develop the skills and mindset to thrive amidst uncertainty.

The pandemic has highlighted the unpredictable nature of the job market. Many individuals who lost their jobs due to industry shutdowns or downsizing had to quickly adapt and find new opportunities. This demonstrated the need for resilience and the ability to embrace change. Those who were able to pivot, acquire new skills, or explore alternative career paths were better positioned to navigate the uncertainties of the job market.

To navigate uncertainties and disruptions effectively,

individuals need to be proactive and future focused. This involves continuously developing new skills and staying informed about industry trends and emerging opportunities. Embracing lifelong learning and adopting a growth mindset is essential in the face of rapidly evolving job requirements and technological advancements.

Networking and building a strong professional network also play a crucial role in navigating uncertainties. Connecting with industry professionals, attending virtual events, and participating in online communities can provide access to valuable insights, mentorship, and potential job opportunities. Building relationships with others who are also navigating uncertainties can offer support and collaboration.

Additionally, cultivating resilience and emotional intelligence is vital. Resilience enables individuals to bounce back from setbacks, adapt to change, and maintain a positive outlook. Emotional intelligence helps individuals manage stress, communicate effectively, and build relationships in challenging circumstances.

In conclusion, the post-pandemic job market is characterized by uncertainties and disruptions. Navigating these challenges requires resilience, adaptability, and a proactive approach. By embracing lifelong learning, staying connected with industry professionals, and cultivating resilience and emotional intelligence, individuals can position themselves to thrive amidst uncertainty. The ability to adapt to changing circumstances, acquire new skills, and seize emerging opportunities will be key in navigating the dynamic job market of the future.

Developing Resilience Skills for Career Success

In this section, we explore the key resilience skills that individuals need to cultivate for career success. Resilience plays a crucial role in overcoming challenges, adapting to change, and bouncing back from setbacks. Developing resilience skills empowers individuals to navigate the ups and downs of their careers and maintain a positive mindset.

Emotional intelligence is an essential resilience skill. It involves recognizing and managing emotions, both in ourselves and others. By developing emotional intelligence, individuals can effectively cope with stress, communicate assertively, and build strong relationships. This skill is particularly valuable in managing conflicts, collaborating with colleagues, and navigating challenging work situations.

Problem-solving is another vital resilience skill. It involves the ability to identify and analyse problems, develop creative solutions, and act. By cultivating problem-solving skills, individuals can approach challenges with a proactive mindset and find innovative ways to overcome obstacles. This skill is highly valued by employers, as it demonstrates resourcefulness and a solution-oriented mindset.

Adaptability is also crucial for career success. The ability to adapt to changing circumstances, embrace new technologies, and learn new skills is vital in today's rapidly evolving work environment. Adaptable individuals are open to change, embrace new challenges, and quickly adjust their strategies when needed. They demonstrate flexibility and a willingness to learn and grow, which are highly valued by employers seeking to navigate uncertainties and disruptions.

Practical strategies can help individuals develop resilience skills. Cultivating a growth mindset, which involves believing in the potential for growth and embracing challenges as opportunities for learning, is key. Seeking support networks, such as mentors, peers, or professional organizations, provides valuable guidance and encouragement during challenging times. Practising self-care, such as maintaining a healthy work-life balance, engaging in activities that promote well-being, and managing stress effectively, is essential for sustaining resilience in the long run.

In conclusion, developing resilience skills is crucial for career success. Emotional intelligence, problem-solving, and adaptability are key resilience skills that empower individuals to navigate challenges and setbacks in their careers. By cultivating these skills, individuals can maintain a positive mindset, embrace change, and proactively overcome obstacles. With resilience, individuals can thrive in today's dynamic work environment and achieve long-term career success.

Adapting to Change and Embracing New Opportunities

In the final part of this chapter, we explore the concept of adaptability and its role in seizing new opportunities in the post-pandemic job market. The COVID-19 pandemic has accelerated changes in industries, job roles, and work environments, requiring individuals to adapt and embrace new opportunities.

Adaptability is the ability to adjust to new circumstances, environments, and technologies. It involves being open to change, learning new skills, and embracing emerging trends. In the fast-paced and ever-evolving job market, adaptable individuals have a competitive advantage. They can quickly respond to shifting needs, take advantage of emerging opportunities, and navigate uncertainties with confidence.

To adapt to change and embrace new opportunities, individuals need to be open to learning and upskilling. Staying current with industry trends, technologies, and best practices is essential. This may involve taking online courses, attending webinars, participating in professional development programs, or seeking mentorship. By continuously expanding their knowledge and skills, individuals can position themselves for success in new and emerging fields.

Identifying emerging opportunities requires keeping a finger on the pulse of the job market. Monitoring industry trends, following market research, and networking with professionals in the field can provide valuable insights. Individuals should seek out areas where demand is growing and align their skills and interests accordingly. This might involve exploring new industries, pivoting to different roles, or leveraging transferable skills in innovative ways.

Embracing new opportunities also requires a willingness to take calculated risks. This might involve starting a new venture, pursuing a passion project, or taking on a challenging assignment. By stepping outside their comfort zone and embracing new experiences, individuals can unlock their full potential and discover unforeseen career opportunities.

In conclusion, adapting to change and embracing new opportunities is essential in the post-pandemic job market. Individuals who are adaptable, open to learning, and willing to take risks are well-positioned to thrive. By staying current with industry trends, continuously upskilling, and identifying emerging opportunities, individuals can navigate uncertainties and disruptions with confidence. By embracing change and seizing new opportunities, individuals can shape a successful and fulfilling career in the dynamic and evolving work landscape.

CHAPTER XXXVII.
THE FUTURE OF LEADERSHIP AND MANAGEMENT

Evolving Leadership Qualities in the Future of Work

In this chapter, we explore the evolving nature of leadership in the post-pandemic job market. The COVID-19 pandemic has brought about significant changes and challenges, requiring leaders to adapt and possess new qualities to navigate the uncertainties and drive success in the future of work.

One of the key qualities that leaders need to possess in the future of work is visionary thinking. In a rapidly changing landscape, leaders must have the ability to envision and articulate a compelling future for their organizations. They need to be forward-thinking, anticipating trends, and identifying opportunities for growth and innovation. By setting a clear vision and inspiring their teams, visionary leaders can drive change and guide their organizations towards success.

Adaptability and agility are also crucial qualities for leaders in the future of work. The ability to pivot, make quick decisions, and adjust strategies in response to unforeseen circumstances is essential. Leaders must be comfortable with ambiguity and uncertainty, embracing change as an opportunity rather than a threat. By being adaptable and agile, leaders can effectively navigate challenges and seize emerging opportunities.

Another important leadership style in the future of work is servant leadership. This approach emphasizes the leader's role in supporting and empowering their team members. Servant leaders prioritize the well-being and growth of their employees, fostering a collaborative and inclusive work environment. They value diverse perspectives, encourage open communication, and empower their teams to take ownership of their work. By adopting a servant leadership mindset, leaders can build strong and engaged teams that drive innovation and achieve collective success.

The example of Elon Musk, CEO of Tesla, and SpaceX, showcases visionary leadership. Musk's ability to push boundaries, inspire his teams, and pursue ambitious goals has led to ground-breaking innovations in the automotive and aerospace industries. His visionary thinking has been a driving force behind the success of his companies.

In conclusion, the future of work requires leaders to possess evolving qualities. Visionary thinking, adaptability, agility, and servant leadership are essential for navigating uncertainties, driving innovation, and fostering a collaborative work environment. By embodying these qualities, leaders can inspire their teams, navigate challenges, and shape a successful future for their organizations in the dynamic and evolving job market.

Leading with Empathy and Emotional Intelligence

In this chapter, we delve into the importance of empathy and emotional intelligence in leadership. The evolving landscape of the post-pandemic job market requires leaders to connect with their teams on a deeper level, foster inclusivity, and create a supportive work environment. Empathy and emotional intelligence are critical qualities that enable leaders to understand and address the needs of their employees.

Empathy is the ability to understand and share the feelings of others. In leadership, empathy is essential for building strong relationships, fostering trust, and creating a sense of belonging. By putting themselves in the shoes of their team members, empathetic leaders can better understand their perspectives, challenges, and aspirations. They can provide support, encouragement, and guidance, which leads to increased engagement and productivity.

Emotional intelligence, on the other hand, refers to the ability to recognize and manage one's own emotions and the emotions of others. Leaders with high emotional intelligence can effectively navigate conflicts, make informed decisions, and respond to challenges with composure and empathy. They are skilled at active listening, recognizing nonverbal cues, and fostering open and honest communication within their teams.

Satya Nadella, CEO of Microsoft, is a prime example of a leader who embodies empathy and emotional intelligence. He has prioritized building a culture of inclusion and psychological safety within Microsoft, which has resulted in high employee satisfaction and innovative solutions. Nadella understands the importance of empathy in driving collaboration and empowering his team members to thrive.

Leaders can develop empathy and emotional intelligence through various strategies. This includes active listening, seeking diverse perspectives, providing constructive feedback, and promoting psychological safety within the team. Investing in leadership development programs and fostering a culture that values empathy and emotional intelligence can have a significant impact on employee engagement, productivity, and overall organizational success.

In conclusion, leading with empathy and emotional intelligence is essential in the post-pandemic job market. By understanding and connecting with their teams on a deeper level, leaders can foster a supportive work environment, drive engagement, and promote innovation. The example of Satya Nadella showcases the positive outcomes that can be achieved by prioritizing empathy and emotional intelligence in leadership. By cultivating these qualities, leaders can inspire their teams and create a positive and inclusive workplace culture.

Adapting Management Styles for a Diverse and Remote Workforce

In this chapter, we address the need for adaptive management styles that cater to the unique challenges and opportunities of a diverse and remote workforce. The post-pandemic job market has brought about significant changes in the way teams collaborate and work together, necessitating leaders to adapt their management approaches to meet the evolving needs of their teams.

Fostering trust is a crucial aspect of managing a diverse and remote workforce. Leaders must establish open lines of communication, encourage transparency, and provide regular feedback to build trust among team members. Trust enables remote employees to feel supported and empowered to take ownership of their work, leading to increased productivity and engagement.

Promoting collaboration is another key component of effective management in a diverse and remote workforce. Leaders should leverage digital tools and platforms to facilitate communication and virtual collaboration, ensuring that team members feel connected and can work together seamlessly despite physical distance. Encouraging regular check-ins, virtual team meetings, and collaborative projects fosters a sense of belonging and teamwork.

Support and resources are vital for the success of remote teams.

Leaders should ensure that remote employees have access to the necessary tools, training, and resources to perform their tasks effectively. Providing clear guidelines and expectations, offering professional development opportunities, and addressing any technical or logistical challenges that remote employees may face are crucial for their success.

Managing a diverse workforce requires cultural sensitivity and inclusive decision-making processes. Leaders should recognize and celebrate diversity, actively seek diverse perspectives, and create an inclusive environment where all voices are heard and valued. By embracing diversity, leaders can tap into a wide range of experiences and ideas, leading to innovation and better problem-solving.

Buffer, a fully remote company, exemplifies an adaptive management style for a remote workforce. They prioritize autonomy, transparency, and clear communication, which enables employees to work flexibly while fostering collaboration and accountability.

In conclusion, adapting management styles for a diverse and remote workforce is essential in the post-pandemic job market. By fostering trust, promoting collaboration, providing support and resources, and embracing diversity, leaders can effectively manage and lead their teams to success. The example of Buffer demonstrates the positive outcomes that can be achieved by implementing an adaptive management approach. By incorporating these strategies, leaders can navigate the challenges and capitalize on the opportunities presented by a diverse and remote workforce, creating a positive and inclusive work environment.

CHAPTER XXXVIII.
THE ROLE OF GOVERNMENT IN SHAPING THE FUTURE OF WORK**

Governments worldwide stand at the helm, guiding their nations through a maze of technological advances, economic shifts, and evolving work paradigms. Their policies, strategies, and collaborations will set the tone for decades to come in the employment sector.

In an ever-changing economic landscape, governments have a crucial role to play in fostering job creation and driving economic growth. This chapter explores the importance of policy initiatives in shaping the future of work by promoting job creation and economic prosperity.

A. Policy initiatives for job creation and economic growth

Governments have the power to implement policies that stimulate job creation and drive economic growth. By strategically investing in infrastructure projects, such as transportation networks, energy systems, and digital connectivity, governments can create employment opportunities while improving the overall business environment.

World Bank data reveals that government-driven infrastructure projects can potentially lead to a 2-3% increase in employment rates in developing nations. These projects not only create jobs directly but also have a multiplier effect on other sectors of the economy, boosting overall economic growth.

Following the 2008 economic recession, the U.S. government launched the American Recovery and Reinvestment Act. This stimulus package aimed to save and create jobs, primarily in the construction and green energy sectors. The investment in infrastructure projects and renewable energy initiatives not only helped revitalize the economy but also fostered the development of sustainable industries.

While technology and automation may lead to job displacements in certain sectors, strategic policy-making that focuses on emerging industries can pave the way for new employment opportunities. Governments can collaborate with private enterprises, research institutions, and educational organizations to identify and support industries with high growth potential. By investing in these sectors and implementing favourable policies, governments can foster innovation, attract investments, and create a conducive environment for job creation and economic growth.

Conclusion

Policy initiatives for job creation and economic growth are crucial in shaping the future of work. By investing in infrastructure, supporting emerging industries, and fostering innovation, governments can create an environment that promotes employment opportunities and economic prosperity. Strategic policymaking is essential to adapt to changing economic trends and leverage emerging technologies for sustainable growth. Through collaboration with various stakeholders, governments can drive economic transformation and ensure a bright future for their citizens.

Ensuring worker protections and social safety nets

As the traditional employee-employer relationship evolves, governments need to adapt their policies to protect workers in diverse forms of employment.

Research conducted by the International Labour Organization reveals that more than 60% of the global workforce is employed in the informal sector, lacking comprehensive protections. These workers often face inadequate wages, unsafe working conditions, and limited access to social protection schemes.

In 2019, Spain introduced a decree granting gig workers, such as those in the food delivery industry, specific rights. This includes the right to unionize and engage in collective bargaining. The aim was to address the vulnerabilities faced by gig workers and provide them with essential protections.

Governments play a crucial role in widening the protective umbrella for workers, regardless of their employment nature. Policies should be enacted to ensure fair wages, access to healthcare, unemployment benefits, and protection against discrimination and exploitation. It is imperative to establish social safety nets that provide a safety net for workers during periods of economic volatility and disruption.

Conclusion:
As the gig economy and flexible employment continue to shape the job market, governments must prioritize worker protection and establish comprehensive social safety nets. The aim should be to ensure that no worker is left unprotected, regardless of their employment nature. By enacting and enforcing legislation,

governments can address the vulnerabilities faced by workers in the informal sector and establish a fair and secure working environment for all. Collaborative efforts involving governments, labour organizations, and businesses are essential in creating policies that promote worker rights and economic stability. Ultimately, a robust system of worker protections and social safety nets contributes to a more equitable and inclusive society.

Collaborations between government, private sector, and education institutions

The collaboration between the government, private sector, and education institutions creates a synergistic environment that aligns education with market demands and equips individuals with the skills needed for the evolving workforce.

Research by the Brookings Institution highlights that public-private partnerships in education can lead to a significant increase in graduation rates in disciplines aligned with market demands. This collaboration ensures that educational programs are relevant and responsive to industry needs.

Germany's dual education system exemplifies successful collaboration between the government, private sector, and education institutions. It combines classroom learning with on-the-job training, supported by both educational institutions and private enterprises. This partnership ensures that students acquire practical skills and knowledge that directly translate into employability.

As the nature of work evolves, the demand for specific skills and competencies changes. Governments, through collaborations, can bridge the gap between education and employment by creating programs that align with industry needs. By involving the private sector and education institutions in curriculum development, internships, and apprenticeships, individuals can gain practical experience and relevant skills that enhance their employability.

Conclusion:
Collaboration between the government, private sector, and education institutions is essential for preparing individuals for the future of work. By aligning education with market demands, fostering partnerships, and integrating practical experience into learning programs, governments can ensure that the workforce is equipped with the necessary skills and competencies. This collaboration ensures that individuals are not only educated but also employable in real-world scenarios. By working together, these three pillars can create a dynamic and resilient workforce that contributes to economic growth and societal development.

CHAPTER XXXIX. FUTURE OF WORK: ETHICAL AND LEGAL CONSIDERATIONS**

Ethical implications of emerging technologies in the workplace

The use of advanced technologies, such as artificial intelligence (AI) and automation, has the potential to enhance productivity and provide valuable insights. However, there are ethical challenges that arise with the implementation of these technologies.

AI algorithms can be biased, leading to potential unfairness in hiring practices or promotions. This bias can be inadvertently introduced due to the data used to train the algorithms, which may reflect historical biases or discrimination.

Amazon's AI recruitment tool serves as a notable example. The tool, based on resumes submitted to the company over a decade, primarily by male candidates, displayed bias against female candidates. This bias was a result of the AI favouring male-oriented language and profiles.

While automation and AI offer numerous benefits, it is crucial to integrate ethical considerations into workplace technologies.

Fairness and transparency should be prioritized to ensure that emerging technologies do not perpetuate biases or discrimination. Human oversight becomes essential to identify and mitigate any unintended consequences arising from these technologies.

Conclusion:
As workplaces embrace emerging technologies, it is imperative to recognize and address the ethical implications associated with their use. Integrating ethical considerations into the development and implementation of workplace technologies will help mitigate biases, promote fairness, and ensure transparency. By maintaining human oversight and actively addressing ethical concerns, organizations can leverage the benefits of emerging technologies while upholding ethical standards and creating a more inclusive and equitable work environment.

Privacy and Data Protection in the Digital Age

In today's digital age, privacy and data protection have become critical considerations in the workplace. With a growing reliance on digital platforms and online communication, organizations must prioritize safeguarding personal and professional data. A study conducted by Cisco revealed that a significant majority, 84% of individuals, value their digital privacy. However, there is a lack of comprehensive understanding among many regarding how their data is used and protected.

One prominent example that highlights the importance of privacy concerns is the case of Zoom. As the pandemic drove a surge in remote work and virtual meetings, Zoom faced substantial criticism over privacy and data security issues. In response, the company took immediate action to strengthen its privacy measures and re-evaluate its protocols. This serves as a reminder that respecting personal boundaries and privacy in virtual workspaces is crucial for building trust and maintaining confidence in digital platforms.

The convergence of personal and professional lives on digital platforms further emphasizes the need for robust privacy and data protection measures. Organizations must prioritize the security of their employee's personal information and ensure responsible handling of data. Transparent communication about data usage and privacy practices is essential for fostering trust among employees and stakeholders. By establishing clear data protection policies, implementing secure technology infrastructure, and providing training on data handling practices, organizations can demonstrate their commitment to privacy and data security.

Maintaining trust through effective data protection measures is crucial for organizations. Mishandling data can lead to severe consequences, including reputational damage and legal repercussions. By recognizing the value of personal and professional data, organizations can create a work environment where employees feel confident that their information is respected and protected.

In conclusion, privacy and data protection are paramount in the digital age. Organizations must prioritize privacy concerns, implement robust security measures, and communicate transparently about data handling practices. Respecting personal boundaries and privacy in virtual workspaces is essential for fostering trust and maintaining a secure and productive work environment. By embracing privacy and data protection, organizations can navigate the digital landscape with confidence and ensure the trust and confidence of their employees and stakeholders.

Legal Frameworks and Regulations for the Future of Work

As the world of work undergoes rapid transformations, it is crucial to reassess and adapt legal frameworks to ensure they remain relevant and effective. With the rise of technologies such as AI and robotics, the global executive community anticipates significant disruptions in employment law, according to a survey by Deloitte. Addressing these challenges requires dynamic legal structures capable of accommodating the changing nature of jobs, rights, and employer-employee relationships.

Deloitte's survey highlights that 79% of global executives expect significant disruptions in employment law due to technological advancements. This includes the integration of AI and robotics into the workforce, which necessitates re-evaluating existing legal frameworks.

California's Assembly Bill 5 (AB5) serves as a prominent case illustrating the need for legal adaptation. AB5 aimed to redefine the gig economy by extending similar rights and protections to gig workers as those enjoyed by full-time employees. However, the legislation sparked widespread debate and required subsequent modifications to address concerns raised by various stakeholders.

The future of work demands legal frameworks that are not only responsive to technological advancements but also prioritize the rights and welfare of workers. It is essential to redefine work and employment relationships to ensure that individuals are not left vulnerable in the wake of digital transformations. Balancing innovation and ethical responsibility are critical to creating inclusive and fair workplaces that foster progress and advancement.

Conclusion:
As we stand at the precipice of a transformative era in the world of work, the convergence of ethics, law, and technology will shape its future. The decisions we make and the legal

frameworks we establish will determine whether we enter an era characterized by inclusivity, fairness, and progress, or face unintended consequences. Striking a balance between innovation and ethical responsibility is fundamental to shaping a future of work that benefits both individuals and society.

CHAPTER XL. WORKFORCE TRANSFORMATION AND FUTURE SKILLS DEVELOPMENT**

Transformative Changes in Job Roles and Skill Requirements

The rapid advancement of technology is bringing about transformative changes in job roles across industries. McKinsey estimates that by 2030, up to 375 million workers may need to transition to entirely new job categories as automation replaces or renders current tasks redundant. However, this shift does not necessarily imply a reduction in jobs but rather a transformation in work and the skills required.

According to McKinsey's research, a significant number of workers will need to adapt to new job roles as automation and technological advancements continue to reshape industries. This highlights the importance of developing skills that are relevant in the future job market.

The banking sector serves as a prime example of how technological advancements have reshaped job roles. In the past, most banking transactions required human intervention.

However, with the emergence of AI-driven chatbots and automated transaction systems, the need for manual intervention has decreased. Nonetheless, there is now a growing demand for AI specialists and data analysts in the banking sector, highlighting the shift towards roles that involve leveraging technology and data.

The changing landscape of work signifies a transition rather than a decline in job opportunities. While automation may replace certain routine tasks, it creates a demand for new roles that require problem-solving, creativity, and the ability to synergize with technology. Embracing these changes and developing skills that align with emerging job roles will be crucial for individuals to thrive in the future job market.

Conclusion:
As technology continues to advance at an unprecedented pace, job roles will continue to evolve. Adapting to these changes requires individuals to continuously update and acquire new skills. Rather than fearing job loss, individuals should embrace the opportunities presented by the transformation of work. By cultivating problem-solving abilities, creativity, and a willingness to adapt, individuals can position themselves for success in the future job market.

Developing Future-Ready Skills for Career Longevity

In a rapidly evolving job market, adaptability and a commitment to lifelong learning are becoming increasingly crucial for long-term career success. As industries undergo transformative changes, individuals must develop future-ready skills to remain competitive and resilient in the face of emerging challenges.

A report by PwC reveals that 77% of CEOs express concern over a shortage of key skills that could potentially hinder their company's growth. This highlights the growing importance of equipping oneself with the right skills to meet the demands of a changing job market.

Atlassian, a renowned enterprise software company, recognized the need to adapt to the evolving software development landscape. To ensure their employees were equipped with the necessary skills, they invested significantly in training programs to upskill their workforce in new technology domains. This proactive approach allowed them to stay ahead of industry trends and maintain a competitive edge.

With industries constantly evolving, relying solely on past achievements is no longer sufficient. Continuous learning and adaptability are not mere buzzwords but essential attributes for career survival in the modern era. Individuals who embrace a growth mindset, are open to learning new skills, and can quickly adapt to changing circumstances will be better positioned to navigate the challenges and seize opportunities that arise.

Conclusion:
To thrive in a rapidly changing job market, individuals must prioritize developing future-ready skills. Employers value employees who can adapt to emerging trends, learn new technologies, and possess a strong foundation of transferable skills. By embracing a mindset of continuous learning, seeking out training and development opportunities, and staying informed about industry advancements, individuals can future-proof their careers and ensure long-term career longevity. In an era of constant disruption, those who are adaptable and committed to acquiring new skills will find doors of opportunity opening before them.

Bridging the Skills Gap through Education and Training

As the world undergoes rapid transformation, bridging the skills gap becomes imperative to prepare the workforce for the future. Traditional education systems alone may not suffice in equipping individuals with the necessary skills for emerging job roles. Collaborative efforts between corporations and educational institutions are essential to bridge the gap between current knowledge and future needs.

According to the World Economic Forum, 65% of children entering primary school today will eventually work in jobs that do not exist yet. This highlights the need to prepare individuals for the evolving nature of work and the emergence of new professions.

IBM's P-TECH (Pathways in Technology Early College High School) initiative exemplifies the collaboration between industry and education. P-TECH merges high school, college, and the world of work through partnerships with industries. This innovative model provides students with both academic and technical skills, ensuring they are job-ready upon graduation.

To bridge the skills gap effectively, it is crucial to foster collaboration between corporations and educational institutions. This partnership can ensure that educational programs align with industry demands, providing students with the skills and knowledge required for future employment. By integrating practical experience, industry insights, and workplace simulations into educational curricula, individuals can acquire the skills and competencies needed to thrive in the evolving job market.

Conclusion:
The transformation of the workforce is not a crisis but an opportunity for growth and progress. By embracing change, fostering continuous learning, and cultivating adaptability, individuals can navigate the shifting landscape of work with confidence. Collaborative efforts between corporations and educational institutions play a vital role in bridging the skills gap and ensuring that the workforce is equipped with the relevant knowledge and abilities. By investing in education

and training programs that align with emerging job roles and technological advancements, we can create a future-ready workforce that drives innovation, economic growth, and societal progress.

CHAPTER XLI. WORKFORCE TRANSFORMATION AND FUTURE SKILLS DEVELOPMENT**

Transformative Changes in Job Roles and Skill Requirements**

The ever-evolving landscape of job roles requires individuals to adapt and acquire new skills to thrive in the future. With the rapid advancements in technology, some job roles are being automated while new ones emerge. Embracing these changes and developing the necessary skills are crucial for success in the evolving job market.

According to the World Economic Forum, by 2025, around 85 million jobs may be displaced due to automation, while 97 million new roles that align with the changing division of labour between humans and machines may emerge. This highlights the significant transformation occurring in the job market.

Automation is reshaping traditional industries. Tesla's car factory in Fremont is a prime example, utilizing over 23,000 robots alongside human workers. Routine tasks like data entry and assembly line work are increasingly automated, creating a demand for roles in data analysis, artificial intelligence, and content creation.

While automation may replace certain job roles, it also presents new opportunities. Uniquely human skills, such as critical thinking, creativity, and complex problem-solving, remain in demand. Rather than viewing technology as a threat, individuals must embrace it as a tool for growth and advancement. Adapting to new technologies and acquiring the necessary skills will be essential for individuals to stay relevant and succeed in the future job market.

Conclusion:
As job roles undergo transformative changes, individuals must be prepared to evolve with them. Embracing technology and acquiring new skills is vital for adapting to the shifting demands of the job market. By focusing on developing skills that are uniquely human, individuals can position themselves for success in roles that complement technological advancements. The key lies in recognizing the opportunities that arise from these transformative changes and continuously upskilling to remain competitive. With the right mindset and a commitment to lifelong learning, individuals can navigate the evolving job market and build a rewarding and fulfilling career.

Developing Future-Ready Skills for Career Longevity

In the rapidly changing world of work, developing future-ready skills is crucial for career longevity and success. Employers increasingly value soft skills such as emotional intelligence, resilience, adaptability, and leadership. Lifelong learning and a proactive approach to skill development have become essential in staying competitive in the job market.

According to LinkedIn's 2020 Workplace Learning Report, 57% of senior leaders believe that soft skills are more critical than hard skills. These skills enable individuals to navigate complex work environments, collaborate effectively, and lead teams. Emotional intelligence, adaptability, and resilience rank high on the list of desired skills.

Google's "Project Aristotle" discovered that the most innovative and productive teams were not necessarily those with the highest IQs, but those that displayed soft skills such as empathy and emotional safety. This demonstrates the importance of interpersonal skills in driving team success.

The pursuit of lifelong learning is no longer a choice but a necessity. Continuous skill development goes beyond formal education and involves self-paced learning, mentorships, and hands-on experiences. Organizations have a role to play by investing in training and development programs that foster the acquisition of future-ready skills. However, individuals also have a responsibility to seek personal growth and take ownership of their skill development.

Conclusion:
To thrive in the ever-changing job market, individuals must prioritize the development of future-ready skills. Soft skills, such as emotional intelligence and adaptability, are increasingly valued by employers and contribute to personal and professional success. Lifelong learning, combined with a proactive approach to skill development, empowers individuals to adapt to new challenges and seize emerging opportunities. By investing in their growth and continuously acquiring new skills, individuals can build career longevity and remain competitive in the dynamic world of work.

Bridging the Skills Gap through Education and Training

In the face of rapid technological advancements, bridging the skills gap has become a pressing concern. The mismatch between the skills individuals possesses and those needed for jobs in the digital world presents a significant challenge. To address this gap, a proactive approach to education and training is necessary.

By 2022, over 54% of employees worldwide will require significant re- and upskilling to meet the demands of emerging job roles and technologies. This highlights the urgency for individuals to acquire new skills and update their knowledge to remain relevant in the evolving job market.

Recognizing the potential skills gap, Amazon launched a $700 million initiative to upskill 100,000 of its employees by 2025. This program aims to help employees transition into more advanced roles within the company, equipping them with the necessary skills to thrive in the digital age.

To bridge the skills gap, traditional educational systems must evolve to incorporate more practical, skills-based learning. The focus should shift from rote memorization to developing critical thinking, problem-solving, and digital literacy. Collaboration between industries and educational institutions is vital. Initiatives like apprenticeships, internships, and specialized training programs can provide individuals with hands-on experience and industry-specific skills, ensuring they are prepared for the changing job landscape.

Conclusion:
The metamorphosis of the workforce demands proactive measures to bridge the skills gap. Individual career longevity and collective progress in industries and economies hinge on our ability to adapt and acquire new skills. From skill awareness to mastery, a commitment to lifelong learning is essential. By embracing education and training opportunities, individuals can stay competitive, organizations can meet their talent needs, and societies can thrive in the face of technological advancements. The journey towards bridging the skills gap is a collective effort that will shape the future of work.

CHAPTER XLII. WORKFORCE TRANSFORMATION AND FUTURE SKILLS DEVELOPMENT

Transformative Changes in Job Roles and Skill Requirements

The job landscape is undergoing transformative changes, driven by technological advancements and global shifts. In this chapter, we explore the impact of these changes on job roles and the skills required for success in the post-pandemic job market.

Technological advancements, automation, and digitalization are reshaping industries and job sectors. According to the World Economic Forum, by 2025, 85 million jobs may be displaced, while 97 million new roles could emerge. This highlights the need for individuals to adapt and acquire new skills to remain competitive.

The rise of artificial intelligence (AI) and machine learning has led to the automation of tasks in various industries. For instance, manufacturing processes are increasingly automated, and customer service is being augmented with AI-powered chatbots. As a result, the demand for skills related to data analysis, programming, and AI expertise is growing.

To thrive in the evolving job market, individuals must possess a range of skills. Critical thinking, problem-solving, and digital literacy have become essential in navigating the digital age. The ability to adapt to new technologies and work in diverse environments is crucial. Additionally, creativity and innovation play a vital role in driving growth and staying ahead of the curve.

As job roles transform, individuals need to embrace lifelong learning to keep their skills up to date. Continuous education and upskilling programs can help individuals bridge the gap between their existing skills and the ones in demand. Collaboration between educational institutions, industry experts, and policymakers is key to ensuring relevant and effective skill development initiatives.

Conclusion:
The transformative changes in job roles and skill requirements present both challenges and opportunities. By recognizing emerging trends, acquiring in-demand skills, and embracing lifelong learning, individuals can navigate the changing job landscape with confidence. The ability to adapt, think critically, and harness technological advancements will be vital for success in the post-pandemic job market. As we move forward, individuals, educational institutions, and industries must work together to foster a workforce that is prepared for the transformative changes that lie ahead.

Developing Future-Ready Skills for Career Longevity

In the rapidly evolving job market, developing future-ready skills is essential for ensuring career longevity and adaptability. In this section, we provide practical guidance on how individuals can equip themselves with the necessary skills to thrive in a changing professional landscape.

Continuous learning and skill development are crucial to staying relevant and competitive. According to the World Economic Forum, by 2022, over half of all employees will require significant reskilling and upskilling. Embracing this reality is vital for long-term career success.

Google's Digital Garage program exemplifies the commitment to developing future-ready skills. This initiative offers free online courses on various digital skills, including data analysis, digital marketing, and web development. By providing accessible and comprehensive training, Google aims to empower individuals with the skills needed for the digital economy.

To develop future-ready skills, individuals must embrace a mindset of continuous learning. This includes seeking opportunities for upskilling and reskilling through various avenues such as online courses, certifications, workshops, and professional networks. These resources can help individuals stay abreast of industry trends, acquire new knowledge, and enhance their expertise.

Additionally, cultivating a growth mindset and adaptability is crucial. Embracing change and being open to acquiring new skills and knowledge will ensure individuals remain competitive and resilient in the face of evolving job requirements.

Collaboration between employers, educational institutions, and individuals is essential in facilitating skill development. Employers can provide training programs and create a culture that supports continuous learning. Educational institutions can offer relevant courses and certifications, while individuals can take ownership of their learning journey and actively seek growth opportunities.

Conclusion:
Developing future-ready skills is essential for career longevity

and adaptability. By embracing continuous learning, upskilling, and reskilling, individuals can navigate the ever-changing job market with confidence. Initiatives like Google's Digital Garage demonstrate the importance of accessible skill development programs. As technology advances and industries evolve, the pursuit of future-ready skills becomes a lifelong endeavour, ensuring individuals remain agile and competitive in their professional journeys.

Bridging the Skills Gap through Education and Training

In this section, we address the challenge of the skills gap and the crucial role of education and training in bridging this gap. We discuss the importance of collaboration between educational institutions, employers, and government agencies to align curricula with industry needs. Additionally, we explore initiatives such as apprenticeships, internships, and vocational training programs that provide practical skills and work experience.

The skills gap refers to the mismatch between the skills that employers require, and the skills possessed by job seekers. Bridging this gap is essential to ensure a competent and well-prepared workforce. According to a survey by ManpowerGroup, 54% of employers globally reported difficulties in filling job vacancies due to the skills gap.

Germany's dual education system serves as a successful model for bridging the skills gap. This system combines classroom learning with on-the-job training, allowing students to gain practical skills and experience while pursuing their education. By aligning curricula with industry needs and providing hands-on training, Germany prepares students for the workforce and bridges the gap between education and industry requirements.

To bridge the skills gap effectively, the collaboration between educational institutions, employers, and government agencies is essential. This collaboration ensures that educational programs are designed to meet the evolving needs of industries. It also helps in identifying emerging skill requirements and incorporating them into curricula.

Initiatives such as apprenticeships, internships, and vocational training programs play a vital role in bridging the skills gap. These programs provide individuals with practical skills, industry exposure, and work experience, making them more job-ready and enhancing their employability.

Conclusion:
Bridging the skills gap is critical for a competent and competitive workforce. Collaboration between educational institutions, employers, and government agencies, along with the implementation of initiatives like apprenticeships and vocational training programs, can help address this challenge. By equipping individuals with the necessary skills and practical experience, we can create a workforce that meets the evolving needs of industries. This chapter emphasizes the importance of education and training in bridging the skills gap and preparing individuals for the future of work.

XLIII. Conclusion: Embracing the Future of Work

Recap of Key Insights and Takeaways

In this final chapter, we summarize the key insights and takeaways from our exploration of the future of work in the post-pandemic job market. We have delved into various aspects of the changing work landscape, including remote work, technological advancements, skill requirements, diversity and inclusion, and leadership. By recapping the main points discussed in each chapter, we aim to reinforce the key learnings and provide a holistic understanding of the future of work.

Remote Work:
The COVID-19 pandemic has accelerated the adoption of remote work. It has highlighted the importance of flexible work arrangements, digital collaboration tools, and effective communication for successful remote work experiences. Remote work offers opportunities for increased work-life balance and access to global talent pools.

Technological Advancements:
Technological advancements, such as AI, automation, and digitalization, are reshaping job roles and skill requirements. While certain jobs may be replaced by automation, new opportunities emerge in areas like data analysis, AI, and content creation. Developing digital literacy, adaptability, and creativity is crucial for career longevity.

Skill Requirements:
Future-ready skills, including critical thinking, problem-solving, emotional intelligence, and digital literacy, are essential for career success. Continuous learning, upskilling, and reskilling are necessary to stay relevant and competitive in the evolving job market. Lifelong learning through online courses, certifications, and professional networks is becoming the norm.

Diversity and Inclusion:
Creating diverse and inclusive workplaces is crucial for innovation and productivity. Embracing diversity in gender, race, age, and perspectives fosters creativity, drives innovation, and enhances decision-making. Organizations must prioritize diversity and inclusion through inclusive hiring practices, fostering an inclusive culture, and providing equal opportunities for growth and development.

Leadership:
Effective leadership in the future of work requires qualities such as adaptability, emotional intelligence, and empathy. Leaders must embrace change, foster collaboration, and empower their

teams. The role of leaders in shaping organizational culture, promoting diversity and inclusion, and driving innovation are vital for success.

Conclusion:
The future of work in the post-pandemic job market is dynamic and ever evolving. Embracing remote work, adapting to technological advancements, developing future-ready skills, fostering diversity and inclusion, and embracing effective leadership are key pillars for success. By understanding and applying these insights, individuals and organizations can navigate the changing landscape and thrive in the future of work. Continuous learning, flexibility, and embracing change will be the foundation for success in the exciting opportunities that lie ahead.

Embracing Change and Staying Adaptable in the Evolving Job Market

We emphasise the importance of embracing change and staying adaptable in the face of evolving job market dynamics. The rapid pace of technological advancements and societal shifts requires individuals to continually update their skills, remain flexible, and adapt to new work environments. By discussing the need for a growth mindset and a willingness to learn and evolve, we provide insights into how individuals can navigate the changing job market and thrive in their careers.

Adapting to Remote Work:
The COVID-19 pandemic catalysed the widespread adoption of remote work. Those who embraced the change and quickly adapted to remote work tools and practices were able to maintain productivity and work-life balance. This shift in mindset allowed individuals to discover new ways of working and opened doors for remote job opportunities. It highlighted the importance of technology literacy, effective communication,

and self-discipline in a remote work setting.

Continuous Learning and Skill Development:
In an evolving job market, continuous learning and skill development are vital. By staying updated with the latest industry trends, individuals can identify emerging skills and areas of growth. This may involve pursuing online courses, attending workshops, participating in professional networks, or seeking mentorship opportunities. A growth mindset and a commitment to lifelong learning enable individuals to adapt to changing job requirements and remain competitive.

Flexibility and Agility:
Being flexible and agile in the workplace allows individuals to navigate shifting demands and seize new opportunities. This may involve taking on new roles, embracing cross-functional projects, or seeking career transitions. The ability to quickly learn and adapt to different work environments, technologies, and organizational cultures enhances one's employability and professional growth.

Seizing Opportunities in Change:
Change often brings opportunities for growth and innovation. By embracing change, individuals can proactively seek out new challenges, projects, and collaborations. They can leverage their adaptability to contribute fresh perspectives, drive change within their organizations, and position themselves for career advancement.

Conclusion:
In the evolving job market, embracing change and staying adaptable is essential for long-term career success. Adapting to remote work, continuous learning, flexibility, and seizing opportunities in change are key strategies for staying ahead in one's professional journey. By cultivating a growth mindset and embracing the evolving nature of work, individuals can navigate the dynamic job market and thrive in their careers.

Inspiring Individuals to Navigate and Thrive in the Future of Work

In closing, we provide inspiration and practical guidance for individuals to navigate and thrive in the future of work. We encourage readers to take ownership of their careers, identify their strengths and passions, and align their work with their values and aspirations. By nurturing their skills, adapting to emerging trends, and embracing change, individuals can position themselves for success in the dynamic and evolving work landscape.

The Power of Continuous Learning:
Continuous learning is a key ingredient for success in the future of work. By staying curious, seeking out new knowledge, and developing new skills, individuals can adapt to changing job requirements and remain relevant in their fields. Embracing a growth mindset allows for personal and professional growth and opens doors to new opportunities.

Building a Strong Professional Network:
A strong professional network is invaluable in navigating the future of work. By fostering connections, seeking mentorship, and participating in industry events, individuals can tap into a wealth of knowledge and potential collaborations. Building relationships with like-minded professionals enhances career prospects and creates a support system for personal and professional development.

Leveraging Personal Branding:
In a competitive job market, personal branding is crucial. By showcasing their unique skills, experiences, and values, individuals can stand out from the crowd and attract opportunities aligned with their aspirations. Embracing authenticity and leveraging digital platforms can amplify their

brand and expand their professional reach.

Inspiring Role Models:
Inspiring figures like Jack Ma, the co-founder of Alibaba Group, serve as examples of navigating the future of work successfully. By recognizing emerging trends and adapting to market demands, he built a thriving business empire and empowered others through his platform. His journey inspires individuals to embrace change, seize opportunities, and continuously evolve.

Conclusion:
This book has explored the future of work in the post-pandemic job market, emphasizing adaptability, continuous learning, and a growth mindset. By embracing change, nurturing their skills, building a strong network, and leveraging personal branding, individuals can navigate and thrive in the evolving work landscape. The future of work holds immense possibilities for those who are proactive, resilient, and willing to seize opportunities. We hope that this book has provided valuable insights and inspiration to help readers navigate their journeys in the future of work and create fulfilling and successful careers.

www.ingramcontent.com/pod-product-compliance
Lightning Source LLC
Chambersburg PA
CBHW072149290526
45794CB00004B/1463